I0164964

GOD'S OWN WORD
ON THE FEAR OF THE LORD

Compiled by Pastor Scott Markle

Shepherding the Flock Ministries

7971 Washington St. ❖ Melvin, MI 48454
(810) 378-5323
www.shepherdingtheflock.com

Copyright © 2013 by Pastor Scott Markle

God's Own Word: On the Fear of the Lord
Compiled by Pastor Scott Markle

Printed in the United States of America

ISBN 9780615903460

All rights reserved solely by the author.

All Bible quotations are from the King James Version of
the Bible.

Shepherding the Flock Ministries
7971 Washington St.
Melvin, MI 48454
(810) 378-5323
www.shepherdingtheflock.com

CONTENTS

INTRODUCTION

The "God's Own Word" booklet series is intended to reveal only God's own Word on a particular matter. Each booklet provides a compilation of Biblical passages on a particular subject and categorizes those passages under a set of headings related to that subject. In addition, portions of each passage are highlighted in bold italics in order to point out the parts of the passage that are the most relevant to the subject. In this manner, the reader is instructed *by God's own Word*. I pray that these booklets may spiritually edify, exhort, and encourage your heart.

For the Excellency of the Knowledge of Christ Jesus our Lord,
Abiding in Christ, and Christ in us,
Pastor Scott Markle

The Fear of the Lord

Genesis 22:1-3, 9-13 - And it came to pass after these things, that God did tempt [test] Abraham, and said unto him, Abraham: and he said, Behold, here I am. And he said, Take now thy son, thine only son Isaac, whom thou lovest, and get thee into the land of Moriah; and offer him there for a burnt offering upon one of the mountains which I will tell thee of. And Abraham rose up early in the morning, and saddled his ass, and took two of his young men with him, and Isaac his son, and clave the wood for the burnt offering, and rose up, and went unto the place of which God had told him . . . . And they came to the place which God had told him of; and Abraham built an altar there, and laid the wood in order, and bound Isaac his son, and laid him on the altar upon the wood. And Abraham stretched forth his hand, and took the knife to slay his son. And the angel of the LORD called unto him out of heaven, and said, Abraham, Abraham: and he said, Here am I. And he said, Lay not thine hand upon the lad, neither do thou any thing unto him: *for now I know that thou fearest God, seeing thou hast not withheld thy son, thine only son from me*. And Abraham lifted up his eyes, and looked, and behold behind him a ram caught in a thicket by his horns: *and Abraham went and took the ram, and offered him up for a burnt offering in the stead of his son*.

Genesis 31:42 - *Except the God of my father, the God of Abraham, and the fear of Isaac*, had been with me, surely thou hadst sent me away now empty. God hath seen mine affliction and the labour of my hands, and rebuked thee yesternight.

Genesis 42:18 - And Joseph said unto them the third day, This do, and live; *for I fear God*.

Exodus 1:15-17 - And the king of Egypt spake to the Hebrew midwives, of which the name of the one was Shiphrah, and the name of the other Puah: and he said, When ye do the office of a midwife to the Hebrew women, and see them upon the stools; if it be a son, then ye shall kill him: but if it be a daughter, then she shall live. *But the midwives feared God, and did not as the king of Egypt commanded them*, but saved the men children alive.

Exodus 9:13-21 - And the LORD said unto Moses, Rise up early in the morning, and stand before Pharaoh, and say unto him, Thus saith the LORD God of the Hebrews, Let my people go, that they may serve me. For I will at this time send all my plagues upon thine heart, and upon thy servants, and upon thy people; *that thou mayest know that there is none like me in all the earth*. For now I will stretch out my hand, that I may smite thee and thy people with pestilence; and thou shalt be cut off from the earth. *And in very deed for this cause have I raised thee up, for to shew in thee my power; and that my name may be declared throughout all the earth*. As yet exaltest thou thyself against my people, that thou wilt not let them go? Behold, to morrow about this time I will cause it to rain a very grievous hail, such as hath not been in Egypt since the foundation thereof even until now. Send therefore now, and gather thy cattle, and all that thou hast in the field; for upon every man and beast which shall be found in the field, and shall not be brought home, the hail shall come down upon them, and they shall die. *He that feared the word of the LORD among the servants of Pharaoh made his servants and his cattle flee into the houses*: and he that regarded not the word of the LORD left his servants and his cattle in the field.

Exodus 18:21 - Moreover thou shalt provide out of all the people *able men, such as fear God, men of truth, hating covetousness*; and place such over them, to be rulers of thousands, and rulers of hundreds, rulers of fifties, and rulers of tens.

Leviticus 19:14 - Thou shalt not curse the deaf, nor put a stumblingblock before the blind, *but shalt fear thy God: I am the LORD*.

Leviticus 19:32 - Thou shalt rise up before the hoary head, and honour the face of the old man, *and fear thy God: I am the LORD*.

Leviticus 25:17, 35-37, 43 - Ye shall not therefore oppress one another; *but thou shalt fear thy God: for I am the LORD your God* . . . . And if thy brother be waxen poor, and fallen in decay with thee; then thou shalt relieve him: yea, though he be a stranger, or a sojourner; that he may live with thee. Take thou no usury of him, or increase: *but fear thy God*; that thy brother may live with thee. Thou shalt not give him thy money upon usury, nor lend him thy victuals for increase . . . . Thou shalt not rule over him with rigour; *but shalt fear thy God*.

Deuteronomy 5:29 - *O that there were such an heart in them, that they would fear me, and keep all my commandments always*, that it might be well with them, and with their children for ever!

Deuteronomy 6:1-25 - *Now these are the commandments, the statutes, and the judgments, which the* LORD *your God commanded to teach you, that ye might do them* in the land whither ye go to possess it: *that thou mightest fear the* LORD *thy God, to keep all his statutes and his commandments, which I command thee, thou, and thy son, and thy son's son, all the days of thy life*; and that thy days may be prolonged. Hear therefore, O Israel, and observe to do it; that it may be well with thee, and that ye may increase mightily, as the LORD God of thy fathers hath promised thee, in the land that floweth with milk and honey. Hear, O Israel: The LORD our God is one LORD: *and thou shalt love the* LORD *thy God with all thine heart, and with all thy soul, and with all thy might. And these words, which I command thee this day, shall be in thine heart: and thou shalt teach them diligently unto thy children, and shalt talk of them when thou sittest in thine house, and when thou walkest by the way, and when thou liest down, and when thou risest up.* And thou shalt bind them for a sign upon thine hand, and they shall be as frontlets between thine eyes. And thou shalt write them upon the posts of thy house, and on thy gates. And it shall be, when the LORD thy God shall have brought thee into the land which he sware unto thy fathers, to Abraham, to Isaac, and to Jacob, to give thee great and goodly cities, which thou buildedst not, and houses full of all good things, which thou filledst not, and wells digged, which thou diggedst not, vineyards and olive trees, which thou plantedst not; when thou shalt have eaten and be full; *then beware lest thou forget the* LORD, which brought thee forth out of the land of Egypt, from the house of bondage. *Thou shalt fear the* LORD *thy God, and serve him, and shalt swear by his name. Ye shall not go after other gods, of the gods of the people which are round about you*; (For the LORD thy God is a jealous God among you) lest the anger of the LORD thy

God be kindled against thee, and destroy thee from off the face of the earth. *Ye shall not tempt the LORD your God, as ye tempted him in Massah. Ye shall diligently keep the commandments of the LORD your God, and his testimonies, and his statutes, which he hath commanded thee. And thou shalt do that which is right and good in the sight of the LORD*: that it may be well with thee, and that thou mayest go in and possess the good land which the LORD sware unto thy fathers, to cast out all thine enemies from before thee, as the LORD hath spoken. And when thy son asketh thee in time to come, saying, What mean the testimonies, and the statutes, and the judgments, which the LORD our God hath commanded you? Then thou shalt say unto thy son, We were Pharaoh's bondmen in Egypt; and the LORD brought us out of Egypt with a mighty hand: and the LORD shewed signs and wonders, great and sore, upon Egypt, upon Pharaoh, and upon all his household, before our eyes: and he brought us out from thence, that he might bring us in, to give us the land which he sware unto our fathers. *And the LORD commanded us to do all these statutes, to fear the LORD our God, for our good always*, that he might preserve us alive, as it is at this day. *And it shall be our righteousness, if we observe to do all these commandments before the LORD our God, as he hath commanded us.*

Deuteronomy 8:1-6 - *All the commandments which I command thee this day shall ye observe to do,* that ye may live, and multiply, and go in and possess the land which the LORD sware unto your fathers. And thou shalt remember all the way which the LORD thy God led thee these forty years in the wilderness, to humble thee, and to prove thee, *to know what was in thine heart, whether thou wouldest keep his commandments, or no.* And he humbled thee, and suffered thee to hunger, and fed thee with manna, which thou knewest not, neither did thy fathers know; that he might make thee know that man doth not live by bread only, ***but by every word that proceedeth out of the mouth of the LORD doth man live.*** Thy raiment waxed not old upon thee, neither did thy foot swell, these forty years. Thou shalt also consider in thine heart, that, as a man chasteneth his son, so the LORD thy God chasteneth thee. ***Therefore thou shalt keep the commandments of the LORD thy God, to walk in his ways, and to fear him.***

Deuteronomy 10:12-21 - ***And now, Israel, what doth the LORD thy God require of thee, but to fear the LORD thy God, to walk in all his ways, and to love him, and to serve the LORD thy God with all thy heart and with all thy soul, to keep the commandments of the LORD, and his statutes, which I command thee this day for thy good?*** Behold, the heaven and the heaven of heavens is the LORD'S thy God, the earth also, with all that therein is. Only the LORD had a delight in thy fathers to love them, and he chose their seed after them, even you above all people, as it is this day. ***Circumcise therefore the foreskin of your heart, and be no more stiffnecked.*** For the LORD your God is God of gods, and Lord of lords, a great God, a mighty, and a terrible, which regardeth not persons, nor taketh reward: he doth execute the judgment of the fatherless and widow, and loveth the stranger, in giving him food and raiment. Love ye therefore the stranger: for ye were strangers in the land of Egypt. ***Thou shalt fear the LORD thy God; him shalt thou serve, and to him shalt thou cleave, and swear by his name. He is thy praise, and he is thy God***, that hath done for thee these great and terrible things, which thine eyes have seen.

Deuteronomy 13:1-5 - If there arise among you a prophet, or a dreamer of dreams, and giveth thee a sign or a wonder, and the sign or the wonder come to pass, whereof he spake unto thee, saying, Let us go after other gods, which thou hast not known, and let us serve them; *thou shalt not hearken unto the words of that prophet, or that dreamer of dreams: for the LORD your God proveth you, to know whether ye love the LORD your God with all your heart and with all your soul. Ye shall walk after the LORD your God, and fear him, and keep his commandments, and obey his voice, and ye shall serve him, and cleave unto him.* And that prophet, or that dreamer of dreams, shall be put to death; *because he hath spoken to turn you away from the LORD your God,* which brought you out of the land of Egypt, and redeemed you out of the house of bondage, *to thrust thee out of the way which the LORD thy God commanded thee to walk in. So shalt thou put the evil away from the midst of thee.*

Joshua 24:14-18 - *Now therefore fear the LORD, and serve him in sincerity and in truth: and put away the gods which your fathers served on the other side of the flood, and in Egypt; and serve ye the LORD.* And if it seem evil unto you to serve the LORD, choose you this day whom ye will serve; whether the gods which your fathers served that were on the other side of the flood, or the gods of the Amorites, in whose land ye dwell: *but as for me and my house, we will serve the LORD. And the people answered and said, God forbid that we should forsake the LORD, to serve other gods*; for the LORD our God, he it is that brought us up and our fathers out of the land of Egypt, from the house of bondage, and which did those great signs in our sight, and preserved us in all the way wherein we went, and among all the people through whom we passed: and the LORD drave out from before us all the people, even the Amorites which dwelt in the land: *therefore will we also serve the LORD; for he is our God.*

1 Samuel 12:14-15, 24-25 - *If ye will fear the LORD, and serve him, and obey his voice, and not rebel against the commandment of the LORD*, then shall both ye and also the king that reigneth over you continue following the LORD your God: *but if ye will not obey the voice of the LORD, but rebel against the commandment of the LORD*, then shall the hand of the LORD be against you, as it was against your fathers . . . . *Only fear the LORD, and serve him in truth with all your heart*: for consider how great things he hath done for you. But if ye shall still do wickedly, ye shall be consumed, both ye and your king.

2 Samuel 23:3 - The God of Israel said, the Rock of Israel spake to me, *He that ruleth over men must be just, ruling in the fear of God.*

1 Kings 18:3-4 - And Ahab called Obadiah, which was the governor of his house. (*Now Obadiah feared the LORD greatly: for it was so, when Jezebel cut off the prophets of the LORD, that Obadiah took an hundred prophets, and hid them by fifty in a cave, and fed them with bread and water.*)

2 Kings 17:35-39 - With whom the LORD had made a covenant, and charged them, saying, *Ye shall not fear other gods, nor bow yourselves to them, nor serve them, nor sacrifice to them: but the LORD, who brought you up out of the land of Egypt with great power and a stretched out arm, him shall ye fear, and him shall ye worship, and to him shall ye do sacrifice. And the statutes, and the or- dinances, and the law, and the commandment, which he wrote for you, ye shall observe to do for evermore; and ye shall not fear other gods. And the covenant that I have made with you ye shall not forget; neither shall ye fear other gods. But the LORD your God ye shall fear*; and he shall deliver you out of the   hand of all your enemies.

2 Chronicles 19:5-11 - And he set judges in the land throughout all the fenced cities of Judah, city by city, and said to the judges, *Take heed what ye do: for ye judge not for man, but for the LORD, who is with you in the judgment. Wherefore now let the fear of the LORD be upon you; take heed and do it*: for there is no iniquity with the LORD our God, nor respect of persons, nor taking of gifts. Moreover in Jerusalem did Jehoshaphat set of the Levites, and of the priests, and of the chief of the fathers of Israel, for the judgment of the LORD, and for controversies, when they returned to Jerusalem. And he charged them, saying, *Thus shall ye do in the fear of the LORD, faithfully, and with a perfect heart.* And what cause soever shall come to you of your brethren that dwell in their cities, between blood and blood, between law and commandment, statutes and judgments, *ye shall even warn them that they trespass not against the LORD, and so wrath come upon you, and upon your brethren: this do, and ye shall not trespass*. And, behold, Amariah the chief priest is over you in all matters of the LORD; and Zebadiah the son of Ishmael, the ruler of the house of Judah, for all the king's matters: also the Levites shall be officers before you. *Deal courageously, and the LORD shall be with the good.*

Nehemiah 1:5-11 - And said, I beseech thee, O LORD God of heaven, the great and terrible God, that keepeth covenant and mercy for them that love him and observe his commandments: let thine ear now be attentive, and thine eyes open, that thou mayest hear the prayer of thy servant, which I pray before thee now, day and night, for the children of Israel thy servants, and confess the sins of the children of Israel, which we have sinned against thee: both I and my father's house have sinned. We have dealt very corruptly against thee, and have not kept the commandments, nor the statutes, nor the judgments, which thou commandedst thy servant Moses. Remember, I beseech thee, the word that thou commandedst thy servant Moses, saying, If ye transgress, I will scatter you abroad among the nations: but if ye turn unto me, and keep my commandments, and do them; though there were of you cast out unto the uttermost part of the heaven, yet will I gather them from thence, and will bring them unto the place that I have chosen to set my name there. Now these are thy servants and thy people, whom thou hast redeemed by thy great power, and by thy strong hand. *O Lord, I beseech thee, let now thine ear be attentive to the prayer of thy servant, and to the prayer of thy servants, who desire to fear thy name*: and prosper, I pray thee, thy servant this day, and grant him mercy in the sight of this man. For I was the king's cupbearer.

Nehemiah 5:6-11, 14-15 - And I was very angry when I heard their cry and these words. Then I consulted with myself, and I rebuked the nobles, and the rulers, and said unto them, *Ye exact usury, every one of his brother*. And I set a great assembly against them. And I said unto them, We after our ability have redeemed our brethren the Jews, which were sold unto the heathen; *and will ye even sell your brethren*? Or shall they be sold unto us? Then held they their peace, and found nothing to answer. Also I said, *It is not good that ye do: ought ye not to walk in the fear of our God because of the reproach of the heathen our enemies?* I likewise, and my brethren, and my servants, might exact of them money and corn: I pray you, let us leave off this usury. *Restore, I pray you, to them, even this day, their lands, their vineyards, their oliveyards, and their houses, also the hundredth part of the money, and of the corn, the wine, and the oil, that ye exact of them* . . . . Moreover from the time that I was appointed to be their governor in the land of Judah, from the twentieth year even unto the two and thirtieth year of Artaxerxes the king, that is, twelve years, I and my brethren have not eaten the bread of the governor. But the former governors that had been before me were chargeable unto the people, and had taken of them bread and wine, beside forty shekels of silver; yea, even their servants bare rule over the people: *but so did not I, because of the fear of God.*

Nehemiah 7:1-2 - Now it came to pass, when the wall was built, and I had set up the doors, and the porters and the singers and the Levites were appointed, that I gave my brother Hanani, and Hananiah the ruler of the palace, charge over Jerusalem: *for he was a faithful man, and feared God above many.*

Job 1:1 - There was a man in the land of Uz, whose name was Job; *and that man was perfect and upright, and one that feared God, and eschewed evil.*

Job 2:3 - And the LORD said unto Satan, *Hast thou considered my servant Job, that there is none like him in the earth, a perfect and an upright man, one that feareth God, and escheweth evil? And still he holdeth fast his integrity*, although thou movedst me against him, to destroy him without cause.

Job 6:14 - *To him that is afflicted pity should be shewed from his friend; but he forsaketh the fear of the Almighty.*

Job 37:23-24 - Touching the Almighty, we cannot find him out: he is excellent in power, and in judgment, and in plenty of justice: he will not afflict. *Men do therefore fear him*: he respecteth not any that are wise of heart.

Psalm 22:23 - *Ye that fear the LORD, praise him; all ye the seed of Jacob, glorify him; and fear him, all ye the seed of Israel.*

Psalm 5:4-7 - For thou art not a God that hath pleasure in wickedness: neither shall evil dwell with thee. The foolish shall not stand in thy sight: thou hatest all workers of iniquity. Thou shalt destroy them that speak leasing: the LORD will abhor the bloody and deceitful man. *But as for me, I will come into thy house in the multitude of thy mercy: and in thy fear will I worship toward thy holy temple.*

Psalm 33:6-11 - By the word of the LORD were the heavens made; and all the host of them by the breath of his mouth. He gathereth the waters of the sea together as an heap: he layeth up the depth in storehouses. *Let all the earth fear the LORD: let all the inhabitants of the world stand in awe of him.* For he spake, and it was done; he commanded, and it stood fast. The LORD bringeth the counsel of the heathen to nought: he maketh the devices of the people of none effect. The counsel of the LORD standeth for ever, the thoughts of his heart to all generations.

Psalm 66:16 - *Come and hear, all ye that fear God, and I will declare what he hath done for my soul.*

Psalm 89:5-14 - *And the heavens shall praise thy wonders, O LORD: thy faithfulness also in the congregation of the saints.* For who in the heaven can be compared unto the LORD? Who among the sons of the mighty can be likened unto the LORD? *God is greatly to be feared in the assembly of the saints, and to be had in reverence of all them that are about him.* O LORD God of hosts, who is a strong LORD like unto thee? Or to thy faithfulness round about thee? Thou rulest the raging of the sea: when the waves thereof arise, thou stillest them. Thou hast broken Rahab in pieces, as one that is slain; thou hast scattered thine enemies with thy strong arm. The heavens are thine, the earth also is thine: as for the world and the fulness thereof, thou hast founded them. The north and the south thou hast created them: Tabor and Hermon shall rejoice in thy name. Thou hast a mighty arm: strong is thy hand, and high is thy right hand. Justice and judgment are the habitation of thy throne: mercy and truth shall go before thy face.

Psalm 96:1-15 - *O sing unto the LORD a new song: sing unto the LORD, all the earth. Sing unto the LORD, bless his name; shew forth his salvation from day to day. Declare his glory among the heathen, his wonders among all people. For the LORD is great, and greatly to be praised: he is to be feared above all gods.* For all the gods of the nations are idols: but the LORD made the heavens. Honour and majesty are before him: strength and beauty are in his sanctuary. *Give unto the LORD, O ye kindreds of the people, give unto the LORD glory and strength. Give unto the LORD the glory due unto his name: bring an offering, and come into his courts. O worship the LORD in the beauty of holiness: fear before him, all the earth. Say among the heathen that the LORD reigneth*: the world also shall be established that it shall not be moved: he shall judge the people righteously. *Let the heavens rejoice, and let the earth be glad; let the sea roar, and the fulness thereof. Let the field be joyful, and all that is therein: then shall all the trees of the wood rejoice before the LORD*: for he cometh, for he cometh to judge the earth: he shall judge the world with righteousness, and the people with his truth.

Psalm 102:15 - *So the heathen shall fear the name of the LORD, and all the kings of the earth thy glory.*

Psalm 118:4 - *Let them now that fear the LORD say, that his mercy endureth for ever.*

Psalm 119:39 - Stablish thy word unto thy servant, *who is devoted to thy fear.*

Psalm 119:63, 74, 79 - *I am a companion of all them that fear thee, and of them that keep thy precepts* . . . . *They that fear thee will be glad when they see me; because I have hoped in thy word* . . . . *Let those that fear thee turn unto me, and those that have known thy testimonies.*

Proverbs 3:5-8 - *Trust in the LORD with all thine heart; and lean not unto thine own understanding. In all thy ways acknowledge him*, and he shall direct thy paths. *Be not wise in thine own eyes: fear the LORD, and depart from evil.* It shall be health to thy navel, and marrow to thy bones.

Proverbs 8:13 - *The fear of the LORD is to hate evil: pride, and arrogancy, and the evil way, and the froward mouth, do I hate.*

Proverbs 14:2 - *He that walketh in his uprightness feareth the LORD*: but he that is perverse in his ways despiseth him.

Proverbs 14:16 - *A wise man feareth, and departeth from evil*: but the fool rageth, and is confident.

Proverbs 23:17-18 - Let not thine heart envy sinners: *but be thou in the fear of the LORD all the day long*. For surely there is an end; and thine expectation shall not be cut off.

Proverbs 24:21-22 - *My son, fear thou the LORD and the king*: and meddle not with them that are given to change: for their calamity shall rise suddenly; and who knoweth the ruin of them both?

Ecclesiastes 12:13 - Let us hear the conclusion of the whole matter: *Fear God, and keep his commandments: for this is the whole duty of man.*

Isaiah 11:1-5 - And there shall come forth a rod out of the stem of Jesse, and a Branch shall grow out of his roots: and the spirit of the LORD shall rest upon him, the spirit of wisdom and understanding, the spirit of counsel and might, *the spirit of knowledge and of the fear of the LORD; and shall make him of quick understanding in the fear of the LORD*: and he shall not judge after the sight of his eyes, neither reprove after the hearing of his ears: but with righteousness shall he judge the poor, and reprove with equity for the meek of the earth: and he shall smite the earth with the rod of his mouth, and with the breath of his lips shall he slay the wicked. And righteousness shall be the girdle of his loins, and faithfulness the girdle of his reins.

Isaiah 50:10 - *Who is among you that feareth the LORD, that obeyeth the voice of his servant*, that walketh in darkness, and hath no light? *Let him trust in the name of the LORD, and stay upon his God.*

Hosea 3:5 - *Afterward shall the children of Israel return, and seek the LORD their God, and David their king; and shall fear the LORD and his goodness in the latter days.*

Jonah 1:9 - And he said unto them, I am an Hebrew; *and I fear the LORD, the God of heaven, which hath made the sea and the dry land.*

Haggai 1:12-13 - Then Zerubbabel the son of Shealtiel, and Joshua the son of Josedech, the high priest, with all the remnant of the people, *obeyed the voice of the LORD their God*, and the words of Haggai the prophet, as the LORD their God had sent him, *and the people did fear before the LORD*. Then spake Haggai the LORD'S messenger in the LORD'S message unto the people, saying, *I am with you, saith the LORD.*

Luke 12:5 - *But I will forewarn you whom ye shall fear: Fear him, which after he hath killed hath power to cast into hell; yea, I say unto you, Fear him.*

Luke 23:39-43 - And one of the malefactors which were hanged railed on him, saying, If thou be Christ, save thyself and us. *But the other answering rebuked him, saying, Dost not thou fear God, seeing thou art in the same condemnation? And we indeed justly; for we receive the due reward of our deeds: but this man hath done nothing amiss. And he said unto Jesus, Lord, remember me when thou comest into thy kingdom.* And Jesus said unto him, Verily I say unto thee, To day shalt thou be with me in paradise.

2 Corinthians 7:1 - Having therefore these promises, dearly beloved, *let us cleanse ourselves from all filthiness of the flesh and spirit, perfecting holiness in the fear of God.*

Ephesians 5:21 - *Submitting yourselves one to another in the fear of God.*

Colossians 3:22-24 - *Servants, obey in all things your masters according to the flesh; not with eyeservice, as menpleasers; but in singleness of heart, fearing God: and whatsoever ye do, do it heartily, as to the Lord, and not unto men; knowing that of the Lord ye shall receive the reward of the inheritance: for ye serve the Lord Christ.*

1 Peter 1:13-17 - *Wherefore gird up the loins of your mind, be sober,* and hope to the end for the grace that is to be brought unto you at the revelation of Jesus Christ; *as obedient children, not fashioning yourselves according to the former lusts in your ignorance*: but as he which hath called you is holy, *so be ye holy in all manner of conversation*; because it is written, *Be ye holy; for I am holy*. And if ye call on the Father, who without respect of persons judgeth according to every man's work, *pass the time of your sojourning here in fear*.

1 Peter 2:17 - Honour all men.   Love the brotherhood. *Fear God.* Honour the king.

Jude 1:22-23 - And of some have compassion, making a difference: *and others save with fear*, pulling them out of the fire; *hating even the garment spotted by the flesh*.

Revelation 14:6-7 - And I saw another angel fly in the midst of heaven, having the everlasting gospel to preach unto them that dwell on the earth, and to every nation, and kindred, and tongue, and people, saying with a loud voice, *Fear God, and give glory to him; for the hour of his judgment is come: and worship him that made heaven, and earth, and the sea, and the fountains of waters*.

Revelation 15:1-4 - And I saw another sign in heaven, great and marvellous, seven angels having the seven last plagues; for in them is filled up the wrath of God. And I saw as it were a sea of glass mingled with fire: and them that had gotten the victory over the beast, and over his image, and over his mark, and over the number of his name, stand on the sea of glass, having the harps of God. And they sing the song of Moses the servant of God, and the song of the Lamb, saying, *Great and marvellous are thy works, Lord God Almighty; just and true are thy ways, thou King of saints. Who shall not fear thee, O Lord, and glorify thy name? For thou only art holy: for all nations shall come and worship before thee; for thy judgments are made manifest*.

Revelation 19:5-7 - And a voice came out of the throne, saying, *Praise our God, all ye his servants, and ye that fear him, both small and great.* And I heard as it were the voice of a great multitude, and as the voice of many waters, and as the voice of mighty thunderings, saying, *Alleluia: for the Lord God omnipotent reigneth. Let us be glad and rejoice, and give honour to him: for the marriage of the Lamb is come, and his wife hath made herself ready.*

The Terror of the Lord Because of His Glory

Psalm 9:19-20 - Arise, O LORD; let not man prevail: let the heathen be judged in thy sight. *Put them in fear, O LORD: that the nations may know themselves to be but men.* Selah.

Hebrews 12:28-29 - Wherefore we receiving a kingdom which cannot be moved, *let us have grace, whereby we may serve God acceptably with reverence and godly fear: for our God is a consuming fire.*

Genesis 28:10-13a, 16-17 - And Jacob went out from Beersheba, and went toward Haran. And he lighted upon a certain place, and tarried there all night, because the sun was set; and he took of the stones of that place, and put them for his pillows, and lay down in that place to sleep. And he dreamed, and behold a ladder set up on the earth, and the top of it reached to heaven: and behold the angels of God ascending and descending on it. *And, behold, the LORD stood above it, and said, I am the LORD God of Abraham thy father, and the God of Isaac* . . . . And Jacob awaked out of his sleep, and he said, *Surely the LORD is in this place*; and I knew it not. *And he was afraid, and said, How dreadful is this place!* This is none other but the house of God, and this is the gate of heaven.

Exodus 3:1-6 - Now Moses kept the flock of Jethro his father in law, the priest of Midian: and he led the flock to the backside of the desert, and came to the mountain of God, even to Horeb. And the angel of the LORD appeared unto him in a flame of fire out of the midst of a bush: and he looked, and, behold, the bush burned with fire, and the bush was not consumed. And Moses said, I will now turn aside, and see this great sight, why the bush is not burnt. And when the LORD saw that he turned aside to see, God called unto him out of the midst of the bush, and said, Moses, Moses. And he said, Here am I. *And he said, Draw not nigh hither: put off thy shoes from off thy feet, for the place whereon thou standest is holy ground. Moreover he said, I am the God of thy father, the God of Abraham, the God of Isaac, and the God of Jacob. And Moses hid his face; for he was afraid to look upon God.*

Exodus 19:16-18 - And it came to pass on the third day in the morning, *that there were thunders and lightnings, and a thick cloud upon the mount, and the voice of the trumpet exceeding loud; so that all the people that was in the camp trembled.* And Moses brought forth the people out of the camp *to meet with God*; and they stood at the nether part of the mount. *And mount Sinai was altogether on a smoke, because the LORD descended upon it in fire: and the smoke thereof ascended as the smoke of a furnace, and the whole mount quaked greatly.*

Deuteronomy 5:4-5 - The LORD talked with you face to face in the mount out of the midst of the fire, (I stood between the LORD and you at that time, to shew you the word of the LORD: *for ye were afraid by reason of the fire*, and went not up into the mount;) saying . . .

Psalm 2:1-12 - Why do the heathen rage, and the people imagine a vain thing? The kings of the earth set themselves, and the rulers take counsel together, against the LORD, and against his anointed, saying, Let us break their bands asunder, and cast away their cords from us. *He that sitteth in the heavens shall laugh: the Lord shall have them in derision. Then shall he speak unto them in his wrath, and vex them in his sore displeasure.* Yet have I set my king upon my holy hill of Zion. I will declare the decree: the LORD hath said unto me, Thou art my Son; this day have I begotten thee. *Ask of me, and I shall give thee the heathen for thine inheritance, and the uttermost parts of the earth for thy possession. Thou shalt break them with a rod of iron; thou shalt dash them in pieces like a potter's vessel.* Be wise now therefore, O ye kings: be instructed, ye judges of the earth. *Serve the LORD with fear, and rejoice with trembling. Kiss the Son, lest he be angry, and ye perish from the way, when his wrath is kindled but a little.* Blessed are all they that put their trust in him.

Psalm 65:5-8 - *By terrible things in righteousness wilt thou answer us, O God of our salvation; who art the confidence of all the ends of the earth, and of them that are afar off upon the sea: which by his strength setteth fast the mountains; being girded with power: which stilleth the noise of the seas, the noise of their waves, and the tumult of the people. They also that dwell in the uttermost parts are afraid at thy tokens: thou makest the outgoings of the morning and evening to rejoice.*

Psalm 76:1-12 - *In Judah is God known: his name is great in Israel.* In Salem also is his tabernacle, and his dwelling place in Zion. *There brake he the arrows of the bow, the shield, and the sword, and the battle.* Selah. Thou art more glorious and excellent than the mountains of prey. The stouthearted are spoiled, they have slept their sleep: and none of the men of might have found their hands. *At thy rebuke, O God of Jacob, both the chariot and horse are cast into a dead sleep. Thou, even thou, art to be feared: and who may stand in thy sight when once thou art angry? Thou didst cause judgment to be heard from heaven; the earth feared, and was still, when God arose to judgment, to save all the meek of the earth.* Selah. Surely the wrath of man shall praise thee: the remainder of wrath shalt thou restrain. *Vow, and pay unto the LORD your God: let all that be round about him bring presents unto him that ought to be feared. He shall cut off the spirit of princes: he is terrible to the kings of the earth.*

Psalm 77:11-20 - I will remember the works of the LORD: surely I will remember thy wonders of old. I will meditate also of all thy work, and talk of thy doings. Thy way, O God, is in the sanctuary: *who is so great a God as our God? Thou art the God that doest wonders: thou hast declared thy strength among the people. Thou hast with thine arm redeemed thy people, the sons of Jacob and Joseph. Selah. The waters saw thee, O God, the waters saw thee; they were afraid: the depths also were troubled. The clouds poured out water: the skies sent out a sound: thine arrows also went abroad. The voice of thy thunder was in the heaven: the lightnings lightened the world: the earth trembled and shook. Thy way is in the sea, and thy path in the great waters, and thy footsteps are not known.* Thou leddest thy people like a flock by the hand of Moses and Aaron.

Psalm 83:1-3, 14-18 - Keep not thou silence, O God: hold not thy peace, and be not still, O God. For, lo, thine enemies make a tumult: and they that hate thee have lifted up the head. They have taken crafty counsel against thy people, and consulted against thy hidden ones . . . . *As the fire burneth a wood, and as the flame setteth the* *mountains on fire; so persecute them with thy tempest, and make them afraid with thy storm. Fill their faces with shame; that they may seek thy name, O LORD. Let them be con-founded and troubled for ever; yea, let them be put to shame, and perish: that men may know that thou, whose name alone is JEHOVAH, art the most high over all the earth.*

Isaiah 2:10-22 - *Enter into the rock, and hide thee in the dust, for fear of the LORD, and for the glory of his majesty. The lofty looks of man shall be humbled, and the haughtiness of men shall be bowed down, and the LORD alone shall be exalted in that day. For the day of the LORD of hosts shall be upon every one that is proud and lofty, and upon every one that is lifted up; and he shall be brought low*: and upon all the cedars of Lebanon, that are high and lifted up, and upon all the oaks of Bashan, and upon all the high mountains, and upon all the hills that are lifted up, and upon every high tower, and upon every fenced wall, and upon all the ships of Tarshish, and upon all pleasant pictures. *And the loftiness of man shall be bowed down, and the haughtiness of men shall be made low: and the LORD alone shall be exalted in that day.* And the idols he shall utterly abolish. And they shall go into the holes of the rocks, and into the caves of the earth, *for fear of the LORD, and for the glory of his majesty, when he ariseth to shake terribly the earth.* In that day a man shall cast his idols of silver, and his idols of gold, which they made each one for himself to worship, to the moles and to the bats; to go into the clefts of the rocks, and into the tops of the ragged rocks, *for fear of the LORD, and for the glory of his majesty, when he ariseth to shake terribly the earth.* Cease ye from man, whose breath is in his nostrils: for wherein is he to be accounted of?

Isaiah 25:1-4 - *O LORD, thou art my God; I will exalt thee, I will praise thy name; for thou hast done wonderful things; thy counsels of old are faithfulness and truth. For thou hast made of a city an heap; of a defenced city a ruin: a palace of strangers to be no city; it shall never be built. Therefore shall the strong people glorify thee, the city of the terrible nations shall fear thee. For thou hast been a strength to the poor, a strength to the needy in his distress, a refuge from the storm, a shadow from the heat, when the blast of the terrible ones is as a storm against the wall.*

Isaiah 59:14-20 - And judgment is turned away backward, and justice standeth afar off: for truth is fallen in the street, and equity cannot enter. Yea, truth faileth; and he that departeth from evil maketh himself a prey: and the LORD saw it, and it displeased him that there was no judgment. And he saw that there was no man, and wondered that there was no intercessor: *therefore his arm brought salvation unto him; and his righteousness, it sustained him. For he put on righteousness as a breastplate, and an helmet of salvation upon his head; and he put on the garments of vengeance for clothing, and was clad with zeal as a cloke. According to their deeds, accordingly he will repay, fury to his adversaries, recompence to his enemies; to the islands he will repay recompence. So shall they fear the name of the LORD from the west, and his glory from the rising of the sun. When the enemy shall come in like a flood, the Spirit of the LORD shall lift up a standard against him. And the Redeemer shall come to Zion, and unto them that turn from transgression in Jacob, saith the LORD.*

Jeremiah 5:20-22 - Declare this in the house of Jacob, and publish it in Judah, saying, Hear now this, O foolish people, and without understanding; which have eyes, and see not; which have ears, and hear not: *Fear ye not me? saith the LORD: will ye not tremble at my presence, which have placed the sand for the bound of the sea by a perpetual decree, that it cannot pass it: and though the waves thereof toss themselves, yet can they not prevail; though they roar, yet can they not pass over it?*

Jeremiah 10:6-7 - *Forasmuch as there is none like unto thee, O LORD; thou art great, and thy name is great in might. Who would not fear thee, O King of nations? For to thee doth it appertain: forasmuch as among all the wise men of the nations, and in all their kingdoms, there is none like unto thee.*

Daniel 6:25-27 - Then king Darius wrote unto all people, nations, and languages, that dwell in all the earth; Peace be multiplied unto you. I make a decree, *That in every dominion of my kingdom men tremble and fear before the God of Daniel: for he is the living God, and stedfast for ever, and his kingdom that which shall not be destroyed, and his dominion shall be even unto the end. He delivereth and rescueth, and he worketh signs and wonders in heaven and in earth, who hath delivered Daniel from the power of the lions.*

Jonah 1:3-4, 9-10, 15-16 - But Jonah rose up to flee unto Tarshish from the presence of the LORD, and went down to Joppa; and he found a ship going to Tarshish: so he paid the fare thereof, and went down into it, to go with them unto Tarshish from the presence of the LORD. *But the LORD sent out a great wind into the sea, and there was a mighty tempest in the sea, so that the ship was like to be broken . . . . And he said unto them, I am an Hebrew; and I fear the LORD, the God of heaven, which hath made the sea and the dry land. Then were the men exceedingly afraid,* and said unto him, Why hast thou done this? For the men knew that he fled from the presence of the LORD, because he had told them . . . . So they took up Jonah, and cast him forth into the sea: *and the sea ceased from her raging. Then the men feared the LORD exceedingly, and offered a sacrifice unto the LORD, and made vows.*

Luke 2:8-9 - And there were in the same country shepherds abiding in the field, keeping watch over their flock by night. And, lo, the angel of the Lord came upon them, *and the glory of the Lord shone round about them: and they were sore afraid.*

Luke 5:18-26 - And, behold, men brought in a bed a man which was taken with a palsy: and they sought means to bring him in, and to lay him before him. And when they could not find by what way they might bring him in because of the multitude, they went upon the housetop, and let him down through the tiling with his couch into the midst before Jesus. And when he saw their faith, he said unto him, *Man, thy sins are forgiven thee.* And the scribes and the Pharisees began to reason, saying, Who is this which speaketh blasphemies? Who can forgive sins, but God alone? But when Jesus perceived their thoughts, he answering said unto them, What reason ye in your hearts? Whether is easier, to say, Thy sins be forgiven thee; or to say, Rise up and walk? *But that ye may know that the Son of man hath power upon earth to forgive sins, (he said unto the sick of the palsy,) I say unto thee, Arise, and take up thy couch, and go into thine house. And immediately he rose up before them, and took up that whereon he lay, and departed to his own house, glorifying God. And they were all amazed, and they glorified God, and were filled with fear, saying, We have seen strange things to day.* (See also Matthew 9:1-8; Mark 2:1-12)

Luke 7:12-16 - Now when he came nigh to the gate of the city, behold, there was a dead man carried out, the only son of his mother, and she was a widow: and much people of the city was with her. And when the Lord saw her, he had compassion on her, and said unto her, Weep not. And he came and touched the bier: and they that bare him stood still. *And he said, Young man, I say unto thee, Arise. And he that was dead sat up, and began to speak.* And he delivered him to his mother. *And there came a fear on all: and they glorified God, saying, That a great prophet is risen up among us; and, That God hath visited his people.*

Mark 4:39-41 - *And he arose, and rebuked the wind, and said unto the sea, Peace, be still. And the wind ceased, and there was a great calm.* And he said unto them, Why are ye so fearful? How is it that ye have no faith? *And they feared exceedingly, and said one to another, What manner of man is this, that even the wind and the sea obey him?*

Luke 8:26-29, 32-35, 37 - And they arrived at the country of the Gadarenes, which is over against Galilee. And when he went forth to land, there met him out of the city a certain man, which had devils long time, and ware no clothes, neither abode in any house, but in the tombs. When he saw Jesus, he cried out, and fell down before him, and with a loud voice said, What have I to do with thee, *Jesus, thou Son of God most high*? I beseech thee, torment me not. (*For he had commanded the unclean spirit to come out of the man.* For oftentimes it had caught him: and he was kept bound with chains and in fetters; and he brake the bands, and was driven of the devil into the wilderness.). . . . And there was there an herd of many swine feeding on the mountain: and they besought him that he would suffer them to enter into them. *And he suffered them. Then went the*

devils out of the man, and entered into the swine: and the herd ran violently down a steep place into the lake, and were choked. *When they that fed them saw what was done, they fled*, and went and told it in the city and in the country. Then they went out to see what was done; and came to Jesus, *and found the man, out of whom the devils were departed, sitting at the feet of Jesus, clothed, and in his right mind: and they were afraid . . . . Then the whole multitude of the country of the Gadarenes round about besought him to depart from them; for they were taken with great fear*: and he went up into the ship, and returned back again. (See also Matthew 8:28-34; Mark 5:1-17)

Matthew 17:5-6 - While he yet spake, behold, a bright cloud overshadowed them: *and behold a voice out of the cloud, which said, This is my beloved Son, in whom I am well pleased; hear ye him. And when the disciples heard it, they fell on their face, and were sore afraid.*

Matthew 27:50-54 - Jesus, when he had cried again with a loud voice, yielded up the ghost. And, behold, the veil of the temple was rent in twain from the top to the bottom; and the earth did quake, and the rocks rent; and the graves were opened; and many bodies of the saints which slept arose, and came out of the graves after his resurrection, and went into the holy city, and appeared unto many. *Now when the centurion, and they that were with him, watching Jesus, saw the earthquake, and those things that were done, they feared greatly, saying, Truly this was the Son of God.*

Acts 22:6-9 - And it came to pass, that, as I made my journey, and was come nigh unto Damascus about noon, *suddenly there shone from heaven a great light round about me. And I fell unto the ground*, and heard a voice saying unto me, Saul, Saul, why persecutest thou me? And

I answered, Who art thou, Lord? And he said unto me, *I am Jesus of Nazareth*, whom thou persecutest. *And they that were with me saw indeed the light, and were afraid*; but they heard not the voice of him that spake to me.

1 Corinthians 2:1-5 - *And I, brethren, when I came to you, came not with excellency of speech or of wisdom, declaring unto you the testimony of God.* For I determined not to know any thing among you, save Jesus Christ, and him crucified. *And I was with you in weakness, and in fear, and in much trembling. And my speech and my preaching was not with enticing words of man's wisdom, but in demonstration of the Spirit and of power*: that your faith should not stand in the wisdom of men, but in the power of God.

2 Corinthians 5:10-11 - *For we must all appear before the judgment seat of Christ*; that every one may receive the things done in his body, according to that he hath done, whether it be good or bad. *Knowing therefore the terror of the Lord, we persuade men*; but we are made manifest unto God; and I trust also are made manifest in your consciences.

Philippians 2:9-13 - *Wherefore God also hath highly exalted him, and given him a name which is above every name: that at the name of Jesus every knee should bow*, of things in heaven, and things in earth, and things under the earth; *and that every tongue should confess that Jesus Christ is Lord, to the glory of God the Father. Wherefore, my beloved, as ye have always obeyed, not as in my presence only, but now much more in my absence, work out your own salvation with fear and trembling.* For it is God which worketh in you both to will and to do of his good pleasure.

The Fear of God's People Because His Hand Is with Them

Genesis 35:1-5 - And God said unto Jacob, Arise, go up to Bethel, and dwell there: and make there an altar unto God, that appeared unto thee when thou fleddest from the face of Esau thy brother. Then Jacob said unto his household, and to all that were with him, Put away the strange gods that are among you, and be clean, and change your garments: and let us arise, and go up to Bethel; and I will make there an altar unto God, who answered me in the day of my distress, and was with me in the way which I went. And they gave unto Jacob all the strange gods which were in their hand, and all their earrings which were in their ears; and Jacob hid them under the oak which was by Shechem. And they journeyed: *and the terror of God was upon the cities that were round about them, and they did not pursue after the sons of Jacob.*

Psalm 105:36-38 - He smote also all the firstborn in their land, the chief of all their strength. He brought them forth also with silver and gold: and there was not one feeble person among their tribes. Egypt was glad when they departed: *for the fear of them fell upon them.*

Exodus 23:20-22, 27 - Behold, I send an Angel before thee, to keep thee in the way, and to bring thee into the place which I have prepared. Beware of him, and obey his voice, provoke him not; for he will not pardon your transgressions: for my name is in him. But if thou shalt indeed obey his voice, and do all that I speak; *then I will be an enemy unto thine enemies, and an adversary unto thine adversaries . . . . I will send my fear before thee, and will destroy all the people to whom thou shalt come, and I will make all thine enemies turn their backs unto thee.*

Exodus 34:29-30 - And it came to pass, when Moses came down from mount Sinai with the two tables of testimony in Moses' hand, when he came down from the mount, *that Moses wist not that the skin of his face shone while he talked with him. And when Aaron and all the children of Israel saw Moses, behold, the skin of his face shone; and they were afraid to come nigh him.*

Numbers 12:1-2, 4, 6-8 - And Miriam and Aaron spake against Moses because of the Ethiopian woman whom he had married: for he had married an Ethiopian woman. And they said, Hath the LORD indeed spoken only by Moses? Hath he not spoken also by us? And the LORD heard it . . . . And the LORD spake suddenly unto Moses, and unto Aaron, and unto Miriam, Come out ye three unto the tabernacle of the congregation. And they three came out . . . . And he said, Hear now my words: If there be a prophet among you, I the LORD will make myself known unto him in a vision, and will speak unto him in a dream. My servant Moses is not so, who is faithful in all mine house. With him will I speak mouth to mouth, even apparently, and not in dark speeches; and the similitude of the LORD shall he behold: *wherefore then were ye not afraid to speak against my servant Moses*?

Deuteronomy 2:25 - *This day will I begin to put the dread of thee and the fear of thee upon the nations that are under the whole heaven, who shall hear report of thee, and shall tremble, and be in anguish because of thee.*

Deuteronomy 11:22-23, 25 - For if ye shall diligently keep all these commandments which I command you, to do them, to love the LORD your God, to walk in all his ways, and to cleave unto him; *then will the LORD drive out all these nations from before you*, and ye shall possess greater nations and mightier than yourselves . . . . *There shall no man be able to stand before you: for the LORD your God shall lay the fear of you and the dread of you upon all the land that ye shall tread upon, as he hath said unto you.*

Deuteronomy 28:1, 7, 9-10 - And it shall come to pass, if thou shalt hearken diligently unto the voice of the LORD thy God, to observe and to do all his commandments which I command thee this day, that the LORD thy God will set thee on high above all nations of the earth . . . . *The LORD shall cause thine enemies that rise up against thee to be smitten before thy face: they shall come out against thee one way, and flee before thee seven ways* . . . . The LORD shall establish thee an holy people unto himself, as he hath sworn unto thee, if thou shalt keep the commandments of the LORD thy God, and walk in his ways. *And all people of the earth shall see that thou art called by the name of the LORD; and they shall be afraid of thee.*

Joshua 4:14 - *On that day the LORD magnified Joshua in the sight of all Israel; and they feared him, as they feared Moses, all the days of his life.*

1 Samuel 18:12-15, 28-29 - *And Saul was afraid of David, because the LORD was with him, and was departed from Saul.* Therefore Saul removed him from him, and made him his captain over a thousand; and he went out and came in before the people. And David behaved himself wisely in all his ways; *and the LORD was with him. Wherefore when Saul saw that he behaved himself very wisely, he was afraid of him* . . . . *And Saul saw and knew that the LORD was with David*, and that Michal Saul's daughter loved him. *And Saul was yet the more afraid of David*; and Saul became David's enemy continually.

1 Chronicles 14:8-17 - And when the Philistines heard that David was anointed king over all Israel, all the Philistines went up to seek David. And David heard of it, and went out against them. And the Philistines came and spread themselves in the valley of Rephaim. And David enquired of God, saying, Shall I go up against the Philistines? *And wilt thou deliver them into mine hand? And the LORD said unto him, Go up; for I will deliver them into thine hand.* So they came up to Baalperazim; and David smote them there. *Then David said, God hath broken in upon mine enemies by mine hand like the breaking forth of waters*: therefore they called the name of that place Baalperazim. And when they had left their gods there, David gave a commandment, and they were burned with fire. And the Philistines yet again spread themselves abroad in the valley. Therefore David enquired again of God; and God said unto him, Go not up after them; turn away from them, and come upon them over against the mulberry trees. And it shall be, when thou shalt hear a sound of going in the tops of the mulberry trees, that then thou shalt go out to battle: *for God is gone forth before thee to smite the host of the Philistines*. David therefore did as God commanded him: and they smote the host of the Philistines from Gibeon even to Gazer. *And the fame of David went out into all lands; and the LORD brought the fear of him upon all nations.*

1 Kings 3:28 - And all Israel heard of the judgment which the king had judged; *and they feared the king: for they saw that the wisdom of God was in him, to do judgment.*

2 Chronicles 14:9, 11-14a - And there came out against them Zerah the Ethiopian with an host of a thousand thousand, and three hundred chariots . . . . *And Asa cried unto the LORD his God, and said, LORD, it is nothing with thee to help, whether with many, or with them that have no power: help us, O LORD our God; for we rest on thee, and in thy name we go against this multitude. O LORD, thou art our God; let not man prevail against thee. So the LORD smote the Ethiopians before Asa, and before Judah*; and the Ethiopians fled. And Asa and the people that were with him pursued them unto Gerar: and the Ethiopians were overthrown, that they could not recover themselves; *for they were destroyed before the LORD, and before his host*; and they carried away very much spoil. And they smote all the cities round about Gerar; *for the fear of the LORD came upon them* . . . .

2 Chronicles 17:3-5a, 10 - *And the LORD was with Jehoshaphat*, because he walked in the first ways of his father David, and sought not unto Baalim; but sought to the LORD God of his father, and walked in his commandments, and not after the doings of Israel. *Therefore the LORD stablished the kingdom in his hand* . . . . *And the fear of the LORD fell upon all the kingdoms of the lands that were round about Judah, so that they made no war against Jehoshaphat.*

Esther 8:17 - And in every province, and in every city, whithersoever the king's commandment and his decree came, *the Jews had joy and gladness, a feast and a good day. And many of the people of the land became Jews; for the fear of the Jews fell   upon them.*

Psalm 18:32-45 - *It is God that girdeth me with strength, and maketh my way perfect. He maketh my feet like hinds' feet, and setteth me upon my high places. He teacheth my hands to war, so that a bow of steel is broken by mine arms. Thou hast also given me the shield of thy salvation: and thy right hand hath holden me up, and thy gentleness hath made me great. Thou hast enlarged my steps under me, that my feet did not slip.* I have pursued mine enemies, and overtaken them: neither did I turn again till they were consumed. I have wounded them that they were not able to rise: they are fallen under my feet. *For thou hast girded me with strength unto the battle: thou hast subdued under me those that rose up against me. Thou hast also given me the necks of mine enemies; that I might destroy them that hate me.* They cried, but there was none to save them: even unto the LORD, but he answered them not. Then did I beat them small as the dust before the wind: I did cast them out as the dirt in the streets. *Thou hast delivered me from the strivings of the people; and thou hast made me the head of the heathen*: a people whom I have not known shall serve me. As soon as they hear of me, they shall obey me: the strangers shall submit themselves unto me. *The strangers shall fade away, and be afraid out of their close places.*

Psalm 48:1-6 - *Great is the LORD, and greatly to be praised in the city of our God, in the mountain of his holiness. Beautiful for situation, the joy of the whole earth, is mount Zion, on the sides of the north, the city of the great King. God is known in her palaces for a refuge.* For, lo, the kings were assembled, they passed by together. *They saw it, and so they marvelled; they were troubled, and hasted away. Fear took hold upon them there, and pain, as of a woman in travail.*

Jeremiah 33:7-9 - And I will cause the captivity of Judah and the captivity of Israel to return, and will build them, as at the first. And I will cleanse them from all their iniquity, whereby they have sinned against me; and I will pardon all their iniquities, whereby they have sinned, and whereby they have transgressed against me. *And it shall be to me a name of joy, a praise and an honour before all the nations of the earth, which shall hear all the good that I do unto them: and they shall fear and tremble for all the goodness and for all the prosperity that I procure unto it.*

Micah 7:14-17 - *Feed thy people with thy rod, the flock of thine heritage,* which dwell solitarily in the wood, in the midst of Carmel: let them feed in Bashan and Gilead, as in the days of old. *According to the days of thy coming out of the land of Egypt will I shew unto him marvellous things. The nations shall see and be confounded at all their might:* they shall lay their hand upon their mouth, their ears shall be deaf. They shall lick the dust like a serpent, they shall move out of their holes like worms of the earth: *they shall be afraid of the LORD our God, and shall fear because of thee.*

Mark 6:20 - *For Herod feared John, knowing that he was a just man and an holy, and observed him;* and when he heard him, he did many things, and heard him gladly.

Learning to Fear the Lord

Exodus 14:31 - *And Israel saw that great work which the LORD did upon the Egyptians: and the people feared the LORD*, and believed the LORD, and his servant Moses.

Exodus 15:11 - Who is like unto thee, O LORD, among the gods? *Who is like thee, glorious in holiness, fearful in praises, doing wonders?*

Exodus 20:18, 20 - And all the people saw the thunderings, and the lightnings, and the noise of the trumpet, and the mountain smoking: and when the people saw it, they removed, and stood afar off . . . . And Moses said unto the people, Fear not: *for God is come to prove you, and that his fear may be before your faces, that ye sin not.*

Deuteronomy 4:9-10 - Only take heed to thyself, and keep thy soul diligently, lest thou forget the things which thine eyes have seen, and lest they depart from thy heart all the days of thy life: but teach them thy sons, and thy sons' sons; *specially the day that thou stoodest before the LORD thy God in Horeb, when the LORD said unto me, Gather me the people together, and I will make them hear my words, that they may learn to fear me all the days that they shall live upon the earth, and that they may teach their children.*

Deuteronomy 8:2-9 - *And thou shalt remember all the way which the LORD thy God led thee these forty years in the wilderness, to humble thee, and to prove thee,* to know what was in thine heart, whether thou wouldest keep his commandments, or no. *And he humbled thee, and suffered thee to hunger, and fed thee with manna,* which thou knewest not, neither did thy fathers know; *that he might make thee know that man doth not live by bread only, but by every word that proceedeth out of the mouth of the LORD doth man live. Thy raiment waxed not old upon thee, neither did thy foot swell, these forty years. Thou shalt also consider in thine heart, that, as a man chasteneth his son, so the LORD thy God chasteneth thee. Therefore thou shalt keep the commandments of the LORD thy God, to walk in his ways, and to fear him. For the LORD thy God bringeth thee into a good land,* a land of brooks of water, of fountains and depths that spring out of valleys and hills; a land of wheat, and barley, and vines, and fig trees, and pomegranates; a land of oil olive, and honey; a land wherein thou shalt eat bread without scarceness, thou shalt not lack any thing in it; a land whose stones are iron, and out of whose hills thou mayest dig brass.

Deuteronomy 14:22-23 - *Thou shalt truly tithe all the increase of thy seed, that the field bringeth forth year by year.* And thou shalt eat before the LORD thy God, in the place which he shall choose to place his name there, the tithe of thy corn, of thy wine, and of thine oil, and the firstlings of thy herds and of thy flocks; that *thou mayest learn to fear the LORD thy God always*.

Deuteronomy 17:18-20 - And it shall be, when he sitteth upon the throne of his kingdom, *that he shall write him a copy of this law in a book out of that which is before the priests the Levites: and it shall be with him, and he shall* *read therein all the days of his life: that he may learn to fear the LORD his God, to keep all the words of this law and these statutes, to do them: that his heart be not lifted up above his brethren, and that he turn not aside from the commandment, to the right hand, or to the left*: to the end that he may prolong his days in his kingdom, he, and his children, in the midst of Israel.

Deuteronomy 31:10-13 - And Moses commanded them, saying, At the end of every seven years, in the solemnity of the year of release, in the feast of tabernacles, when all Israel is come to appear before the LORD thy God in the place which he shall choose, *thou shalt read this law before all Israel in their hearing. Gather the people together, men, and women, and children, and thy stranger that is within thy gates, that they may hear, and that they may learn, and fear the LORD your God, and observe to do all the words of this law: and that their children, which have not known any thing, may hear, and learn to fear the LORD your God*, as long as ye live in the land whither ye go over Jordan to possess it.

Joshua 4:20-24 - And those twelve stones, which they took out of Jordan, did Joshua pitch in Gilgal. And he spake unto the children of Israel, saying, When your children shall ask their fathers in time to come, saying, What mean these stones? Then ye shall let your children know, saying, Israel came over this Jordan on dry land. For the LORD your God dried up the waters of Jordan from before you, until ye were passed over, as the LORD your God did to the Red sea, which he dried up from before us, until we were gone over: *that all the people of the earth might know the hand of the LORD, that it is mighty: that ye might fear the LORD your God for ever*.

1 Samuel 12:23-25 - Moreover as for me, God forbid that I should sin against the LORD in ceasing to pray for you: *but I will teach you the good and the right way*: only fear the LORD, and serve him in truth with all your heart: *for consider how great things he hath done for you*. But if ye shall still do wickedly, ye shall be consumed, both ye and your king.

1 Kings 8:38-43 - What prayer and supplication soever be made by any man, or by all thy people Israel, which shall know every man the plague of his own heart, and spread forth his hands toward this house: *then hear thou in heaven thy dwelling place, and forgive, and do, and give to every man according to his ways, whose heart thou knowest*; (for thou, even thou only, knowest the hearts of all the children of men;) *that they may fear thee all the days that they live* in the land which thou gavest unto our fathers. Moreover concerning a stranger, that is not of thy people Israel, but cometh out of a far country for thy name's sake; (*For they shall hear of thy great name, and of thy strong hand, and of thy stretched out arm*;) when he shall come and pray toward this house; *hear thou in heaven thy dwelling place, and do according to all that the stranger calleth to thee for: that all people of the earth may know thy name, to fear thee, as do thy people Israel*; and that they may know that this house, which I have builded, is called by thy name.

Psalm 19:7-9 - *The law of the LORD* is perfect, converting the soul: *the testimony of the LORD* is sure, making wise the simple. *The statutes of the LORD* are right, rejoicing the heart: *the commandment of the LORD* is pure, enlightening the eyes. *The fear of the LORD* is clean, enduring for ever: *the judgments of the LORD* are true and righteous altogether.

Psalm 22:23-24 - Ye that fear the LORD, praise him; all ye the seed of Jacob, glorify him; *and fear him, all ye the seed of Israel. For he hath not despised nor abhorred the affliction of the afflicted; neither hath he hid his face from him; but when he cried unto him, he heard.*

Psalm 34:11-22 - Come, ye children, hearken unto me: *I will teach you the fear of the LORD.* What man is he that desireth life, and loveth many days, that he may see good? *Keep thy tongue from evil, and thy lips from speaking guile. Depart from evil, and do good; seek peace, and pursue it.* The eyes of the LORD are *upon the righteous*, and his ears are open unto their cry. The face of the LORD is against them that do evil, to cut off the remembrance of them from the earth. *The righteous cry*, and the LORD heareth, and delivereth them out of all their troubles. The LORD is nigh unto them that are *of a broken heart*; and saveth such as be *of a contrite spirit.* Many are the afflicttions *of the righteous*: but the LORD delivereth him out of them all. He keepeth all his bones: not one of them is broken. Evil shall slay the wicked: and they that hate the righteous shall be desolate. The LORD redeemeth the soul *of his servants*: and none *of them that trust in him* shall be desolate.

Psalm 40:1-3 - I waited patiently for the LORD; and he inclined unto me, and heard my cry. *He brought me up also out of an horrible pit, out of the miry clay, and set my feet upon a rock, and established my goings. And he hath put a new song in my mouth, even praise unto our God: many shall see it, and fear, and shall trust in the LORD.*

Psalm 52:1-9 - Why boastest thou thyself in mischief, O mighty man? The goodness of God endureth continually. Thy tongue deviseth mischiefs; like a sharp razor, working deceitfully. Thou lovest evil more than good; and lying rather than to speak righteousness. Selah. Thou lovest all devouring words, O thou deceitful tongue. *God shall likewise destroy thee for ever, he shall take thee away, and pluck thee out of thy dwelling place, and root thee out of the land of the living.* Selah. *The righteous also shall see, and fear, and shall laugh at him*: Lo, this is the man that made not God his strength; but trusted in the abundance of his riches, and strengthened himself in his wickedness. But I am like a green olive tree in the house of God: I trust in the mercy of God for ever and ever. I will praise thee for ever, because thou hast done it: and I will wait on thy name; for it is good before thy saints.

Psalm 64:3-10 - Who whet their tongue like a sword, and bend their bows to shoot their arrows, even bitter words: that they may shoot in secret at the perfect: suddenly do they shoot at him, and fear not. They encourage themselves in an evil matter: they commune of laying snares privily; they say, Who shall see them? They search out in-iquities; they accomplish a diligent search: both the inward thought of every one of them, and the heart, is deep. *But God shall shoot at them with an arrow; suddenly shall they be wounded. So they shall make their own tongue to fall upon themselves: all that see them shall flee away. And all men shall fear, and shall declare the work of God; for they shall wisely consider of his doing. The righteous shall be glad in the LORD, and shall trust in him; and all the upright in heart shall glory.*

Psalm 67:5-7 - *Let the people praise thee, O God; let all the people praise thee. Then shall the earth yield her increase; and God, even our own God, shall bless us. God shall bless us; and all the ends of the earth shall fear him.*

Psalm 86:11 - *Teach me thy way, O LORD; I will walk in thy truth: unite my heart to fear thy name.*

Psalm 130:4 - *But there is forgiveness with thee, that thou mayest be feared.*

Proverbs 2:1-9 - *My son, if thou wilt receive my words, and hide my commandments with thee; so that thou incline thine ear unto wisdom, and apply thine heart to understanding; yea, if thou criest after knowledge, and liftest up thy voice for understanding; if thou seekest her as silver, and searchest for her as for hid treasures; then shalt thou understand the fear of the LORD, and find the knowledge of God.* For the LORD giveth wisdom: out of his mouth cometh knowledge and understanding. He layeth up sound wisdom for the righteous: he is a buckler to them that walk uprightly. He keepeth the paths of judgment, and preserveth the way of his saints. Then shalt thou understand righteousness, and judgment, and equity; yea, every good path.

Ecclesiastes 3:14 - *I know that, whatsoever God doeth, it shall be for ever: nothing can be put to it, nor any thing taken from it: and God doeth it, that men should fear before him.*

Isaiah 29:18-19, 22-24 - And in that day shall the deaf hear the words of the book, and the eyes of the blind shall see out of obscurity, and out of darkness. The meek also shall increase their joy in the LORD, and the poor among men shall rejoice in the Holy One of Israel . . . . Therefore thus saith the LORD, who redeemed Abraham, concerning the house of Jacob, Jacob shall not now be ashamed, neither shall his face now wax pale. *But when he seeth his children, the work of mine hands, in the midst of him, they shall sanctify my name, and sanctify the Holy One of Jacob, and shall fear the God of Israel.* They also that erred in spirit shall come to understanding, and they that murmured shall learn doctrine.

Jeremiah 32:37-41 - Behold, I will gather them out of all countries, whither I have driven them in mine anger, and in my fury, and in great wrath; and I will bring them again unto this place, and I will cause them to dwell safely: ***and they shall be my people, and I will be their God: and I will give them one heart, and one way, that they may fear me for ever, for the good of them, and of their children after them: and I will make an everlasting covenant with them, that I will not turn away from them, to do them good; but I will put my fear in their hearts, that they shall not depart from me.*** Yea, I will rejoice over them to do them good, and I will plant them in this land assuredly with my whole heart and with my whole soul.

Zephaniah 3:1-2, 6-7 - Woe to her that is filthy and polluted, to the oppressing city! She obeyed not the voice; she received not correction; she trusted not in the LORD; she drew not near to her God . . . . ***I have cut off the nations: their towers are desolate; I made their streets waste, that none passeth by: their cities are destroyed, so that there is no man, that there is none inhabitant. I said, Surely thou wilt fear me, thou wilt receive instruction; so their dwelling should not be cut off, howsoever I punished them***: but they rose early, and corrupted all their doings.

The Benefits of Fearing the Lord

Exodus 1:17, 20-21 - But the midwives feared God, and did not as the king of Egypt commanded them, but saved the men children alive . . . . *Therefore God dealt well with the midwives*: and the people multiplied, and waxed very mighty. *And it came to pass, because the midwives feared God, that he made them houses.*

Deuteronomy 6:1-3, 24-25 - Now these are the commandments, the statutes, and the judgments, which the LORD your God commanded to teach you, that ye might do them in the land whither ye go to possess it: that thou mightest fear the LORD thy God, to keep all his statutes and his commandments, which I command thee, thou, and thy son, and thy son's son, all the days of thy life; *and that thy days may be prolonged.* Hear therefore, O Israel, and observe to do it; that it may be well with thee, *and that ye may increase mightily, as the LORD God of thy fathers hath promised thee, in the land that floweth with milk and honey* . . . . And the LORD commanded us to do all these statutes, to fear the LORD our God, *for our good always, that he might preserve us alive, as it is at this day. And it shall be our righteousness*, if we observe to do all these commandments before the LORD our God, as he hath commanded us.

Deuteronomy 5:29 - O that there were such an heart in them, that they would fear me, and keep all my commandments always, *that it might be well with them, and with their children for ever*!

Deuteronomy 17:19-20 - And it shall be with him, and he shall read therein all the days of his life: that he may learn to fear the LORD his God, to keep all the words of this law and these statutes, to do them: that his heart be not lifted up above his brethren, and that he turn not aside from the commandment, to the right hand, or to the left: *to the end that he may prolong his days in his kingdom, he, and his children, in the midst of Israel.*

2 Kings 4:1-7 - Now there cried a certain woman of the wives of the sons of the prophets unto Elisha, saying, *Thy servant my husband is dead; and thou knowest that thy servant did fear the LORD: and the creditor is come to take unto him my two sons to be bondmen.* And Elisha said unto her, What shall I do for thee? Tell me, what hast thou in the house? And she said, Thine handmaid hath not any thing in the house, save a pot of oil. Then he said, Go, borrow thee vessels abroad of all thy neighbours, even empty vessels; borrow not a few. And when thou art come in, thou shalt shut the door upon thee and upon thy sons, and shalt pour out into all those vessels, and thou shalt set aside that which is full. So she went from him, and shut the door upon her and upon her sons, who brought the vessels to her; and she poured out. *And it came to pass, when the vessels were full, that she said unto her son, Bring me yet a vessel. And he said unto her, There is not a vessel more.* And the oil stayed. Then she came and told the man of God. *And he said, Go, sell the oil, and pay thy debt, and live thou and thy children of the rest.*

2 Kings 17:39 - But the L ORD your God ye shall fear; *and he shall deliver you out of the hand of all your enemies.*

Job 1:8-10 - And the L ORD said unto Satan, *Hast thou considered my servant Job, that there is none like him in the earth, a perfect and an upright man, one that feareth God, and escheweth evil?* Then Satan answered the L ORD, and said, *Doth Job fear God for nought? Hast not thou made an hedge about him, and about his house, and about all that he hath on every side? Thou hast blessed the work of his hands, and his substance is increased in the land.*

Job 28:28 - *And unto man he said, Behold, the fear of the Lord, that is wisdom; and to depart from evil is under-standing.*

Psalm 15:2, 4a - He that walketh uprightly, and worketh righteousness, and speaketh the truth in his heart . . . . In whose eyes a vile person is contemned; *but he honoureth them that fear the L ORD.*

Psalm 25:12-14 - What man is he that feareth the L ORD? *Him shall he teach in the way that he shall choose. His soul shall dwell at ease; and his seed shall inherit the earth. The secret of the L ORD is with them that fear him; and he will shew them his covenant.*

Psalm 31:19-24 - *Oh how great is thy goodness, which thou hast laid up for them that fear thee; which thou hast wrought for them that trust in thee before the sons of men! Thou shalt hide them in the secret of thy presence from the pride of man: thou shalt keep them secretly in a pavilion from the strife of tongues.* Blessed be the L ORD: *for he hath shewed me his marvellous kindness in a strong city.* For I said in my haste, I am cut off from before thine eyes: nevertheless thou heardest the voice of my supplications when I cried unto thee. O love the LORD, all ye his saints: *for the LORD preserveth the faithful*, and plenty-fully rewardeth the proud doer. Be of good courage, *and he shall strengthen your heart, all ye that hope in the LORD.*

Psalm 33:18-22 - *Behold, the eye of the LORD is upon them that fear him, upon them that hope in his mercy; to deliver their soul from death, and to keep them alive in famine.* Our soul waiteth for the LORD: *he is our help and our shield.* For our heart shall rejoice in him, because we have trusted in his holy name. *Let thy mercy, O LORD, be upon us, according as we hope in thee.*

Psalm 34:7-10 - *The angel of the LORD encampeth round about them that fear him, and delivereth them.* O taste and see that the LORD is good: *blessed is the man that trusteth in him.* O fear the LORD, ye his saints: *for there is no want to them that fear him.* The young lions do lack, and suffer hunger: *but they that seek the LORD shall not want any good thing.*

Psalm 60:4 - *Thou hast given a banner to them that fear thee, that it may be displayed because of the truth.* Selah.

Psalm 85:8-9 - I will hear what God the LORD will speak: *for he will speak peace unto his people, and to his saints*: but let them not turn again to folly. *Surely his salvation is nigh them that fear him; that glory may dwell in our land.*

Psalm 103:8-18 - *The LORD is merciful and gracious, slow to anger, and plenteous in mercy. He will not always chide: neither will he keep his anger for ever. He hath not dealt with us after our sins; nor rewarded us according to our iniquities. For as the heaven is high above the* *earth, so great is his mercy toward them that fear him.* As far as the east is from the west, so far hath he removed our transgressions from us. Like as a father pitieth his children, so the LORD pitieth them that fear him. For he knoweth our frame; he remembereth that we are dust. As for man, his days are as grass: as a flower of the field, so he flourisheth. For the wind passeth over it, and it is gone; and the place thereof shall know it no more. *But the mercy of the LORD is from everlasting to everlasting upon them that fear him, and his righteousness unto children's children; to such as keep his covenant, and to those that remember his commandments to do them.*

Psalm 111:1-10 - Praise ye the LORD. I will praise the LORD with my whole heart, in the assembly of the upright, and in the congregation. The works of the LORD are great, sought out of all them that have pleasure therein. His work is honourable and glorious: and his righteousness endureth for ever. He hath made his wonderful works to be remembered: *the LORD is gracious and full of compassion. He hath given meat unto them that fear him: he will ever be mindful of his covenant. He hath shewed his people the power of his works, that he may give them the heritage of the heathen.* The works of his hands are verity and judgment; all his commandments are sure. They stand fast for ever and ever, and are done in truth and uprightness. *He sent redemption unto his people: he hath commanded his covenant for ever*: holy and reverend is his name. *The fear of the LORD is the beginning of wisdom: a good understanding have all they that do his commandments*: his praise endureth for ever.

Psalm 115:11, 13 - *Ye that fear the LORD, trust in the LORD: he is their help and their shield .... He will bless them that fear the LORD, both small and great.*

Psalm 112:1-10 - Praise ye the LORD. *Blessed is the man that feareth the LORD, that delighteth greatly in his commandments. His seed shall be mighty upon earth: the generation of the upright shall be blessed. Wealth and riches shall be in his house: and his righteousness endureth for ever. Unto the upright there ariseth light in the darkness*: he is gracious, and full of compassion, and righteous. A good man sheweth favour, and lendeth: he will guide his affairs with discretion. *Surely he shall not be moved for ever: the righteous shall be in everlasting remembrance. He shall not be afraid of evil tidings: his heart is fixed, trusting in the LORD. His heart is established, he shall not be afraid, until he see his desire upon his enemies.* He hath dispersed, he hath given to the poor; *his righteousness endureth for ever; his horn shall be exalted with honour.* The wicked shall see it, and be grieved; he shall gnash with his teeth, and melt away: the desire of the wicked shall perish.

Psalm 128:1-6 - *Blessed is every one that feareth the LORD; that walketh in his ways. For thou shalt eat the labour of thine hands: happy shalt thou be, and it shall be well with thee. Thy wife shall be as a fruitful vine by the sides of thine house: thy children like olive plants round about thy table. Behold, that thus shall the man be blessed that feareth the LORD. The LORD shall bless thee out of Zion: and thou shalt see the good of Jerusalem all the days of thy life. Yea, thou shalt see thy children's children, and peace upon Israel.*

Psalm 145:18-20 - *The LORD is nigh unto all them that call upon him, to all that call upon him in truth. He will fulfil the desire of them that fear him: he also will hear their cry, and will save them. The LORD preserveth all them that love him*: but all the wicked will he destroy.

Psalm 147:11 - *The L*ORD *taketh pleasure in them that fear him, in those that hope in his mercy.*

Proverbs 1:7 - *The fear of the L*ORD *is the beginning of knowledge*: but fools despise wisdom and instruction.

Proverbs 9:10 - *The fear of the L*ORD *is the beginning of wisdom: and the knowledge of the holy is understanding.*

Proverbs 10:27 - *The fear of the L*ORD *prolongeth days*: but the years of the wicked shall be shortened.

Proverbs 13:13 - Whoso despiseth the word shall be destroyed: *but he that feareth the commandment shall be rewarded.*

Proverbs 14:26-27 - *In the fear of the L*ORD *is strong confidence: and his children shall have a place of refuge. The fear of the L*ORD *is a fountain of life, to depart from the snares of death.*

Proverbs 15:16 - *Better is little with the fear of the L*ORD *than great treasure and trouble therewith.*

Proverbs 15:33 - *The fear of the L*ORD *is the instruction of wisdom; and before honour is humility.*

Proverbs 16:6 - By mercy and truth iniquity is purged: *and by the fear of the L*ORD *men depart from evil.*

Proverbs 19:23 - *The fear of the L*ORD *tendeth to life: and he that hath it shall abide satisfied; he shall not be visited with evil.*

Proverbs 28:13-14 - He that covereth his sins shall not prosper: *but whoso confesseth and forsaketh them shall have mercy. Happy is the man that feareth alway*: but he that hardeneth his heart shall fall into mischief.

Proverbs 22:4 - *By humility and the fear of the LORD are riches, and honour, and life.*

Proverbs 31:30-31 - Favour is deceitful, and beauty is vain: *but a woman that feareth the LORD, she shall be praised. Give her of the fruit of her hands; and let her own works praise her in the gates.*

Ecclesiastes 8:12-13 - Though a sinner do evil an hundred times, and his days be prolonged, *yet surely I know that it shall be well with them that fear God, which fear before him*: but it shall not be well with the wicked, neither shall he prolong his days, which are as a shadow; because he feareth not before God.

Isaiah 33:5-6 - The LORD is exalted; for he dwelleth on high: *he hath filled Zion with judgment and righteousness. And wisdom and knowledge shall be the stability of thy times, and strength of salvation: the fear of the LORD is his treasure.*

Isaiah 66:2, 5 - For all those things hath mine hand made, and all those things have been, saith the LORD: *but to this man will I look, even to him that is poor and of a contrite spirit, and trembleth at my word . . . . Hear the word of the LORD, ye that tremble at his word*; Your brethren that hated you, that cast you out for my name's sake, said, Let the LORD be glorified: *but he shall appear to your joy*, and they shall be ashamed.

Malachi 3:16-17 - *Then they that feared the LORD spake often one to another: and the LORD hearkened, and heard it, and a book of remembrance was written before him for them that feared the LORD, and that thought upon his name. And they shall be mine, saith the LORD of hosts, in* *that day when I make up my jewels; and I will spare them, as a man spareth his own son that serveth him.*

Malachi 4:1-3 - For, behold, the day cometh, that shall burn as an oven; and all the proud, yea, and all that do wickedly, shall be stubble: and the day that cometh shall burn them up, saith the LORD of hosts, that it shall leave them neither root nor branch. *But unto you that fear my name shall the Sun of righteousness arise with healing in his wings; and ye shall go forth, and grow up as calves of the stall. And ye shall tread down the wicked; for they shall be ashes under the soles of your feet in the day that I shall do this, saith the LORD of hosts.*

Luke 1:50 - *And his mercy is on them that fear him from generation to generation.*

Acts 9:31 - Then had the churches rest throughout all Judaea and Galilee and Samaria, and were edified; *and walking in the fear of the Lord, and in the comfort of the Holy Ghost, were multiplied.*

Acts 10:1-2, 34-35 - There was a certain man in Caesarea called Cornelius, a centurion of the band called the Italian band, *a devout man, and one that feared God with all his house, which gave much alms to the people, and prayed to God always* . . . . Then Peter opened his mouth, and said, Of a truth I perceive that God is no respecter of persons: *but in every nation he that feareth him, and worketh righteousness, is accepted with him.*

Acts 13:16, 26 - Then Paul stood up, and beckoning with his hand said, Men of Israel, *and ye that fear God*, give audience . . . . Men and brethren, children of the stock of Abraham, *and whosoever among you feareth God, to you is the word of this salvation sent.*

Revelation 11:18 - And the nations were angry, and thy wrath is come, and the time of the dead, that they should be judged, *and that thou shouldest give reward unto thy servants the prophets, and to the saints, and them that fear thy name, small and great*; and shouldest destroy them which destroy the earth.

If You Will Not Fear the Lord

Exodus 9:24, 27-30 - So there was hail, and fire mingled with the hail, very grievous, such as there was none like it in all the land of Egypt since it became a nation . . . . And Pharaoh sent, and called for Moses and Aaron, and said unto them, *I have sinned this time: the LORD is righteous, and I and my people are wicked.* Intreat the LORD (for it is enough) that there be no more mighty thunderings and hail; and I will let you go, and ye shall stay no longer. And Moses said unto him, As soon as I am gone out of the city, I will spread abroad my hands unto the LORD; and the thunder shall cease, neither shall there be any more hail; *that thou mayest know how that the earth is the LORD'S. But as for thee and thy servants, I know that ye will not yet fear the LORD God.*

Deuteronomy 25:17-19 - Remember what Amalek did unto thee by the way, when ye were come forth out of Egypt; how he met thee by the way, *and smote the hind-most of thee, even all that were feeble behind thee, when thou wast faint and weary; and he feared not God.* Therefore it shall be, when the LORD thy God hath given thee rest from all thine enemies round about, in the land which the LORD thy God giveth thee for an inheritance to possess it, *that thou shalt blot out the remembrance of Amalek from under heaven*; thou shalt not forget it.

Deuteronomy 28:58-59 - *If thou wilt not observe to do all the words of this law that are written in this book, that thou mayest fear this glorious and fearful name, THE LORD THY GOD; then the LORD will make thy plagues wonderful, and the plagues of thy seed, even great plagues, and of long continuance, and sore sicknesses, and of long continuance.*

Judges 6:1, 6-10 - *And the children of Israel did evil in the sight of the LORD: and the LORD delivered them into the hand of Midian seven years* . . . . *And Israel was greatly impoverished because of the Midianites*; and the children of Israel cried unto the LORD. And it came to pass, when the children of Israel cried unto the LORD because of the Midianites, that the LORD sent a prophet unto the children of Israel, which said unto them, Thus saith the LORD God of Israel, I brought you up from Egypt, and brought you forth out of the house of bondage; and I delivered you out of the hand of the Egyptians, and out of the hand of all that oppressed you, and drave them out from before you, and gave you their land; *and I said unto you, I am the LORD your God; fear not the gods of the Amorites, in whose land ye dwell: but ye have not obeyed my voice.*

2 Kings 17:7-20 - *For so it was, that the children of Israel had sinned against the LORD their God*, which had brought them up out of the land of Egypt, from under the hand of Pharaoh king of Egypt, *and had feared other gods, and walked in the statutes of the heathen*, whom the LORD cast out from before the children of Israel, and of the kings of Israel, which they had made. *And the children of Israel did secretly those things that were not right against the LORD their God*, and they built them high places in all their cities, from the tower of the watchmen to the fenced city. *And they set them up images and groves in every high*

hill, and under every green tree: and there they burnt incense in all the high places, as did the heathen whom the
LORD carried away before them; and wrought wicked
things to provoke the LORD to anger: for they served
idols, whereof the LORD had said unto them, Ye shall not
do this thing. Yet the LORD testified against Israel, and
against Judah, by all the prophets, and by all the seers,
saying, Turn ye from your evil ways, and keep my commandments and my statutes, according to all the law which
I commanded your fathers, and which I sent to you by my
servants the prophets. *Notwithstanding they would not
hear, but hardened their necks, like to the neck of their
fathers, that did not believe in the LORD their God. And
they rejected his statutes, and his covenant that he made
with their fathers, and his testimonies which he testified
against them; and they followed vanity, and became vain,
and went after the heathen that were round about them,
concerning whom the LORD had charged them, that they
should not do like them. And they left all the commandments of the LORD their God, and made them molten
images, even two calves, and made a grove, and wor-
shipped all the host of heaven, and served Baal. And they
caused their sons and their daughters to pass through the
fire, and used divination and enchantments, and sold
themselves to do evil in the sight of the LORD, to provoke
him to anger. Therefore the LORD was very angry with
Israel, and removed them out of his sight: there was none
left but the tribe of Judah only. Also Judah kept not the
commandments of the LORD their God, but walked in the
statutes of Israel which they made. And the LORD
rejected all the seed of Israel, and afflicted them, and delivered them into the hand of spoilers, until he had cast
them out of his sight.*

2 Kings 17:24-25, 28-29, 32-34 - And the king of Assyria brought men from Babylon, and from Cuthah, and from Ava, and from Hamath, and from Sepharvaim, and placed them in the cities of Samaria instead of the children of Israel: and they possessed Samaria, and dwelt in the cities thereof. *And so it was at the beginning of their dwelling there, that they feared not the LORD: therefore the LORD sent lions among them, which slew some of them* . . . . Then one of the priests whom they had carried away from Samaria came and dwelt in Bethel, *and taught them how they should fear the LORD. Howbeit every nation made gods of their own, and put them in the houses of the high places which the Samaritans had made*, every nation in their cities wherein they dwelt . . . . *So they feared the LORD, and made unto themselves of the lowest of them priests of the high places, which sacrificed for them in the houses of the high places. They feared the LORD, and served their own gods, after the manner of the nations whom they carried away from thence. Unto this day they do after the former manners: they fear not the LORD, neither do they after their statutes, or after their ordinances, or after the law and commandment which the LORD commanded the children of Jacob, whom he named Israel.*

Psalm 36:1-4, 12 - *The transgression of the wicked saith within my heart, that there is no fear of God before his eyes. For he flattereth himself in his own eyes, until his iniquity be found to be hateful. The words of his mouth are iniquity and deceit: he hath left off to be wise, and to do good. He deviseth mischief upon his bed; he setteth himself in a way that is not good; he abhorreth not evil . . . . There are the workers of iniquity fallen: they are cast down, and shall not be able to rise.*

Psalm 55:19-23 - *God shall hear, and afflict them, even he that abideth of old.* Selah. *Because they have no changes, therefore they fear not God. He hath put forth his hands against such as be at peace with him: he hath broken his covenant. The words of his mouth were smoother than butter, but war was in his heart: his words were softer than oil, yet were they drawn swords.* Cast thy burden upon the LORD, and he shall sustain thee: he shall never suffer the righteous to be moved. *But thou, O God, shalt bring them down into the pit of destruction: bloody and deceitful men shall not live out half their days*; but I will trust in thee.

Proverbs 1:20, 22-32 - Wisdom crieth without; she uttereth her voice in the streets . . . How long, ye simple ones, will ye love simplicity? And the scorners delight in their scorning, and fools hate knowledge? Turn you at my reproof: behold, I will pour out my spirit unto you, I will make known my words unto you. Because I have called, and ye refused; I have stretched out my hand, and no man regarded; but ye have set at nought all my counsel, and would none of my reproof: *I also will laugh at your calamity; I will mock when your fear cometh; when your fear cometh as desolation, and your destruction cometh as a whirlwind; when distress and anguish cometh upon you. Then shall they call upon me, but I will not answer; they shall seek me early, but they shall not find me: for that they hated knowledge, and did not choose the fear of the LORD: they would none of my counsel: they despised all my reproof. Therefore shall they eat of the fruit of their own way, and be filled with their own devices. For the turning away of the simple shall slay them, and the prosperity of fools shall destroy them.*

Ecclesiastes 8:12-13 - *Though a sinner do evil an hundred times, and his days be prolonged*, yet surely I know that it shall be well with them that fear God, which fear before him: *but it shall not be well with the wicked, neither shall he prolong his days, which are as a shadow; because he feareth not before God.*

Isaiah 29:13-14 - *Wherefore the Lord said, Forasmuch as this people draw near me with their mouth, and with their lips do honour me, but have removed their heart far from me, and their fear toward me is taught by the precept of men: therefore, behold, I will proceed to do a marvellous work among this people, even a marvellous work and a wonder: for the wisdom of their wise men shall perish, and the understanding of their prudent men shall be hid.*

Jeremiah 2:19 - *Thine own wickedness shall correct thee, and thy backslidings shall reprove thee: know therefore and see that it is an evil thing and bitter, that thou hast forsaken the* LORD *thy God, and that my fear is not in thee, saith the Lord* GOD *of hosts.*

Jeremiah 3:6-9 - The LORD said also unto me in the days of Josiah the king, Hast thou seen that which backsliding Israel hath done? She is gone up upon every high mountain and under every green tree, and there hath played the harlot. And I said after she had done all these things, Turn thou unto me. But she returned not. *And her treacherous sister Judah saw it.* And I saw, when for all the causes whereby backsliding Israel committed adultery I had put her away, and given her a bill of divorce; *yet her treacherous sister Judah feared not, but went and played the harlot also. And it came to pass through the lightness of her whoredom, that she defiled the land, and committed adultery with stones and with stocks.*

Jeremiah 5:23-25 - *But this people hath a revolting and a rebellious heart; they are revolted and gone. Neither say they in their heart, Let us now fear the LORD our God, that giveth rain, both the former and the latter, in his season: he reserveth unto us the appointed weeks of the harvest. Your iniquities have turned away these things, and your sins have withholden good things from you.*

Jeremiah 44:7-12 - Therefore now thus saith the LORD, the God of hosts, the God of Israel; *Wherefore commit ye this great evil against your souls, to cut off from you man and woman, child and suckling, out of Judah, to leave you none to remain; in that ye provoke me unto wrath with the works of your hands, burning incense unto other gods in the land of Egypt, whither ye be gone to dwell, that ye might cut yourselves off, and that ye might be a curse and a reproach among all the nations of the earth?* Have ye forgotten the wickedness of your fathers, and the wickedness of the kings of Judah, and the wickedness of their wives, and your own wickedness, and the wickedness of your wives, which they have committed in the land of Judah, and in the streets of Jerusalem? *They are not humbled even unto this day, neither have they feared, nor walked in my law, nor in my statutes, that I set before you and before your fathers. Therefore thus saith the LORD of hosts, the God of Israel; Behold, I will set my face against you for evil, and to cut off all Judah. And I will take the remnant of Judah, that have set their faces to go into the land of Egypt to sojourn there, and they shall all be consumed, and fall in the land of Egypt; they shall even be consumed by the sword and by the famine: they shall die, from the least even unto the greatest, by the sword and by the famine: and they shall be an execration, and an astonishment, and a curse, and a reproach.*

Malachi 1:6-8, 10b - A son honoureth his father, and a servant his master: *if then I be a father, where is mine honour? And if I be a master, where is my fear? saith the* LORD *of hosts unto you, O priests, that despise my name.* And ye say, Wherein have we despised thy name? *Ye offer polluted bread upon mine altar;* and ye say, Wherein have we polluted thee? *In that ye say, The table of the* LORD *is contemptible. And if ye offer the blind for sacrifice, is it not evil?* And if ye offer the lame and sick, is it not evil? Offer it now unto thy governor; will he be pleased with thee, or accept thy person? saith the LORD of hosts . . . . *I have no pleasure in you, saith the* LORD *of hosts, neither will I accept an offering at your hand.*

Malachi 3:5 - *And I will come near to you to judgment; and I will be a swift witness against* the sorcerers, and against the adulterers, and against false swearers, and against those that oppress the hireling in his wages, the widow, and the fatherless, and that turn aside the stranger from his right, *and fear not me, saith the* LORD *of hosts.*

Romans 3:10-19 - As it is written, There is none righteous, no, not one: there is none that understandeth, there is none that seeketh after God. They are all gone out of the way, they are together become unprofitable; there is none that doeth good, no, not one. Their throat is an open sepulchre; with their tongues they have used deceit; the poison of asps is under their lips: whose mouth is full of cursing and bitterness: their feet are swift to shed blood: destruction and misery are in their ways: and the way of peace have they not known: *there is no fear of God before their eyes.* Now we know that what things soever the law saith, it saith to them who are under the law: *that every mouth may be stopped, and all the world may become guilty before God.*

The Terror of the Lord Because of Our Sin

Genesis 3:8-11 - And they heard the voice of the LORD God walking in the garden in the cool of the day: *and Adam and his wife hid themselves from the presence of the LORD God amongst the trees of the garden.* And the LORD God called unto Adam, and said unto him, Where art thou? *And he said, I heard thy voice in the garden, and I was afraid, because I was naked; and I hid myself.* And he said, Who told thee that thou wast naked? *Hast thou eaten of the tree, whereof I commanded thee that thou shouldest not eat?*

Deuteronomy 9:16-19 - *And I looked, and, behold, ye had sinned against the LORD your God, and had made you a molten calf: ye had turned aside quickly out of the way which the LORD had commanded you.* And I took the two tables, and cast them out of my two hands, and brake them before your eyes. And I fell down before the LORD, as at the first, forty days and forty nights: I did neither eat bread, nor drink water, because of all your sins which ye sinned, in doing wickedly in the sight of the LORD, to provoke him to anger. *For I was afraid of the anger and hot displeaseure, wherewith the LORD was wroth against you to destroy you.* But the LORD hearkened unto me at that time also.

Deuteronomy 13:6-11 - If thy brother, the son of thy mother, or thy son, or thy daughter, or the wife of thy bosom, or thy friend, which is as thine own soul, entice thee secretly, saying, Let us go and serve other gods, which thou hast not known, thou, nor thy fathers; namely, of the gods of the people which are round about you, nigh unto thee, or far off from thee, from the one end of the earth even unto the other end of the earth; thou shalt not consent unto him, nor hearken unto him; *neither shall thine eye pity him, neither shalt thou spare, neither shalt thou conceal him: but thou shalt surely kill him; thine hand shall be first upon him to put him to death, and afterwards the hand of all the people. And thou shalt stone him with stones, that he die; because he hath sought to thrust thee away from the LORD thy God*, which brought thee out of the land of Egypt, from the house of bondage. *And all Israel shall hear, and fear, and shall do no more any such wickedness as this is among you.*

Deuteronomy 17:12-13 - *And the man that will do presumptuously, and will not hearken unto the priest that standeth to minister there before the LORD thy God, or unto the judge, even that man shall die: and thou shalt put away the evil from Israel. And all the people shall hear, and fear, and do no more presumptuously.*

Deuteronomy 19:16-21 - If a false witness rise up against any man to testify against him that which is wrong; then both the men, between whom the controversy is, shall stand before the LORD, before the priests and the judges, which shall be in those days; and the judges shall make diligent inquisition: and, behold, if the witness be a false witness, and hath testified falsely against his brother; *then shall ye do unto him, as he had thought to have done unto his brother: so shalt thou put the evil away from among you.*

And those which remain shall hear, and fear, and shall henceforth commit no more any such evil among you. And thine eye shall not pity; but life shall go for life, eye for eye, tooth for tooth, hand for hand, foot for foot.

Deuteronomy 21:18-21 - If a man have a stubborn and rebellious son, which will not obey the voice of his father, or the voice of his mother, and that, when they have chastened him, will not hearken unto them: then shall his father and his mother lay hold on him, and bring him out unto the elders of his city, and unto the gate of his place; and they shall say unto the elders of his city, This our son is stubborn and rebellious, he will not obey our voice; he is a glutton, and a drunkard. *And all the men of his city shall stone him with stones, that he die: so shalt thou put evil away from among you; and all Israel shall hear, and fear.*

1 Samuel 12:16-19 - Now therefore stand and see this great thing, which the LORD will do before your eyes. Is it not wheat harvest to day? I will call unto the LORD, and he shall send thunder and rain; *that ye may perceive and see that your wickedness is great, which ye have done in the sight of the LORD, in asking you a king.* So Samuel called unto the LORD; and the LORD sent thunder and rain that day: *and all the people greatly feared the LORD and Samuel. And all the people said unto Samuel, Pray for thy servants unto the LORD thy God, that we die not: for we have added unto all our sins this evil, to ask us a king.*

2 Samuel 6:2-3, 6-7, 9 - And David arose, and went with all the people that were with him from Baale of Judah, to bring up from thence the ark of God, whose name is called by the name of the LORD of hosts that dwelleth between the cherubims. *And they set the ark of God upon a new cart*, and brought it out of the house of Abinadab that was in Gibeah: *and Uzzah and Ahio, the sons of Abinadab, drave* *the new cart . . . . And when they came to Nachon's threshingfloor, Uzzah put forth his hand to the ark of God, and took hold of it; for the oxen shook it. And the anger of the LORD was kindled against Uzzah; and God smote him there for his error; and there he died by the ark of God . . . . And David was afraid of the LORD that day,* and said, How shall the ark of the LORD come to me?

1 Chronicles 21:1, 7, 15-18, 26-30 - And Satan stood up against Israel, and provoked David to number Israel . . . . And God was displeased with this thing; therefore he smote Israel . . . . And God sent an angel unto Jerusalem to destroy it: and as he was destroying, the LORD beheld, and he repented him of the evil, and said to the angel that destroyed, It is enough, stay now thine hand. And the angel of the LORD stood by the threshingfloor of Ornan the Jebusite. *And David lifted up his eyes, and saw the angel of the LORD stand between the earth and the heaven, having a drawn sword in his hand stretched out over Jerusalem. Then David and the elders of Israel, who were clothed in sackcloth, fell upon their faces.* And David said unto God, Is it not I that commanded the people to be numbered? *Even I it is that have sinned and done evil indeed*; but as for these sheep, what have they done? Let thine hand, I pray thee, O LORD my God, be on me, and on my father's house; but not on thy people, that they should be plagued. Then the angel of the LORD com-manded Gad to say to David, that David should go up, and set up an altar unto the LORD in the threshingfloor of Ornan the Jebusite . . . . And David built there an altar unto the LORD, and offered burnt offerings and peace offerings, and called upon the LORD; and he answered him from heaven by fire upon the altar of burnt offering. And the LORD commanded the angel; and he put up his sword again into the sheath thereof. At that time when David saw that the LORD had answered him in the threshingfloor of Ornan the Jebusite, then he sacrificed there. For the tabernacle of the LORD, which Moses made in the wilderness, and the altar of the burnt offering, were at that season in the high place at Gibeon. But David could not go before it to enquire of God: *for he was afraid because of the sword of the angel of the LORD.*

Psalm 14:4-5 - *Have all the workers of iniquity no knowledge? Who eat up my people as they eat bread, and call not upon the LORD. There were they in great fear*: for God is in the generation of the righteous.

Psalm 90:7-9, 11 - *For we are consumed by thine anger, and by thy wrath are we troubled. Thou hast set our iniquities before thee, our secret sins in the light of thy countenance. For all our days are passed away in thy wrath*: we spend our years as a tale that is told . . . . *Who knoweth the power of thine anger? Even according to thy fear, so is thy wrath.*

Psalm 119:118-120 - *Thou hast trodden down all them that err from thy statutes*: for their deceit is falsehood. *Thou puttest away all the wicked of the earth like dross*: therefore I love thy testimonies. *My flesh trembleth for fear of thee; and I am afraid of thy judgments.*

Isaiah 13:6-9 - *Howl ye; for the day of the LORD is at hand; it shall come as a destruction from the Almighty. Therefore shall all hands be faint, and every man's heart shall melt: and they shall be afraid: pangs and sorrows shall take hold of them; they shall be in pain as a woman that travaileth: they shall be amazed one at another; their faces shall be as flames. Behold, the day of the LORD cometh, cruel both with wrath and fierce anger, to lay the land desolate: and he shall destroy the sinners thereof out of it.*

Isaiah 19:1-3, 16-17 - The burden of Egypt. *Behold, the LORD rideth upon a swift cloud, and shall come into Egypt: and the idols of Egypt shall be moved at his presence, and the heart of Egypt shall melt in the midst of it.* And I will set the Egyptians against the Egyptians: and they shall fight every one against his brother, and every one against his neighbour; city against city, and kingdom against kingdom. *And the spirit of Egypt shall fail in the midst thereof*; and I will destroy the counsel thereof: and they shall seek to the idols, and to the charmers, and to them that have familiar spirits, and to the wizards . . . . *In that day shall Egypt be like unto women: and it shall be afraid and fear because of the shaking of the hand of the LORD of hosts, which he shaketh over it. And the land of Judah shall be a terror unto Egypt, every one that maketh mention thereof shall be afraid in himself, because of the counsel of the LORD of hosts, which he hath determined against it.*

Jeremiah 2:12-13 - *Be astonished, O ye heavens, at this, and be horribly afraid, be ye very desolate, saith the LORD. For my people have committed two evils; they have forsaken me the fountain of living waters, and hewed them out cisterns, broken cisterns, that can hold no water.*

Habakkuk 3:2 - *O LORD, I have heard thy speech, and was afraid: O LORD, revive thy work* in the midst of the years, in the midst of the years make known; *in wrath remember mercy*.

Acts 5:1-11 - But a certain man named Ananias, with Sapphira his wife, sold a possession, and kept back part of the price, his wife also being privy to it, and brought a certain part, and laid it at the apostles' feet. *But Peter said, Ananias, why hath Satan filled thine heart to lie to the*

Holy Ghost, and to keep back part of the price of the land? Whiles it remained, was it not thine own? And after it was sold, was it not in thine own power? Why hast thou conceived this thing in thine heart? ***Thou hast not lied unto men, but unto God. And Ananias hearing these words fell down, and gave up the ghost: and great fear came on all them that heard these things.*** And the young men arose, wound him up, and carried him out, and buried him. And it was about the space of three hours after, when his wife, not knowing what was done, came in. And Peter answered unto her, Tell me whether ye sold the land for so much? And she said, Yea, for so much. ***Then Peter said unto her, How is it that ye have agreed together to tempt the Spirit of the Lord?*** Behold, the feet of them which have buried thy husband are at the door, and shall carry thee out. ***Then fell she down straightway at his feet, and yielded up the ghost***: and the young men came in, and found her dead, and, carrying her forth, buried her by her husband. ***And great fear came upon all the church, and upon as many as heard these things.***

Acts 19:13-20 - Then certain of the vagabond Jews, exorcists, took upon them to call over them which had evil spirits the name of the Lord Jesus, saying, We adjure you by Jesus whom Paul preacheth. And there were seven sons of one Sceva, a Jew, and chief of the priests, which did so. And the evil spirit answered and said, Jesus I know, and Paul I know; but who are ye? And the man in whom the evil spirit was leaped on them, and overcame them, and prevailed against them, so that they fled out of that house naked and wounded. ***And this was known to all the Jews and Greeks also dwelling at Ephesus; and fear fell on them all, and the name of the Lord Jesus was magnified. And many that believed came, and confessed, and shewed their deeds. Many of them also which used curious arts***

79

brought their books together, and burned them before all men: and they counted the price of them, and found it fifty thousand pieces of silver. *So mightily grew the word of God and prevailed.*

2 Corinthians 11:2-3 - *For I am jealous over you with godly jealousy*: for I have espoused you to one husband, that I may present you as a chaste virgin to Christ. *But I fear, lest by any means, as the serpent beguiled Eve through his subtilty, so your minds should be corrupted from the simplicity that is in Christ.*

2 Corinthians 12:20-21 - *For I fear, lest, when I come, I shall not find you such as I would, and that I shall be found unto you such as ye would not: lest there be debates, envyings, wraths, strifes, backbitings, whisperings, swellings, tumults: and lest, when I come again, my God will humble me among you, and that I shall bewail many which have sinned already, and have not repented of the uncleanness and fornication and lasciviousness which they have committed.*

Galatians 4:8-11 - Howbeit then, when ye knew not God, ye did service unto them which by nature are no gods. But now, after that ye have known God, or rather are known of God, *how turn ye again to the weak and beggarly elements, whereunto ye desire again to be in bondage?* Ye observe days, and months, and times, and years. *I am afraid of you, lest I have bestowed upon you labour in vain.*

1 Timothy 5:20 - *Them that sin rebuke before all, that others also may fear.*

Hebrews 4:1 - *Let us therefore fear, lest, a promise being left us of entering into his rest, any of you should seem to come short of it.*

Hebrews 10:26-31 - *For if we sin wilfully after that we have received the knowledge of the truth*, there remaineth no more sacrifice for sins, *but a certain fearful looking for of judgment and fiery indignation, which shall devour the adversaries.* He that despised Moses' law died without mercy under two or three witnesses: *of how much sorer punishment, suppose ye, shall he be thought worthy, who hath trodden under foot the Son of God, and hath counted the blood of the covenant, wherewith he was sanctified, an unholy thing, and hath done despite unto the Spirit of grace? For we know him that hath said, Vengeance belongeth unto me, I will recompense, saith the Lord. And again, The Lord shall judge his people. It is a fearful thing to fall into the hands of the living God.*

Hebrews 11:7 - *By faith Noah, being warned of God of things not seen as yet, moved with fear, prepared an ark to the saving of his house*; by the which he condemned the world, and became heir of the righteousness which is by faith.

Revelation 18:1-2, 5, 9-11, 15-20 - And after these things I saw another angel come down from heaven, having great power; and the earth was lightened with his glory. And he cried mightily with a strong voice, saying, Babylon the great is fallen, is fallen, and is become the habitation of devils, and the hold of every foul spirit, and a cage of every unclean and hateful bird . . . . *For her sins have reached unto heaven, and God hath remembered her iniquities .... And the kings of the earth, who have committed fornication and lived deliciously with her, shall bewail her, and lament for her, when they shall see the smoke of her* *burning, standing afar off for the fear of her torment, saying, Alas, alas, that great city Babylon, that mighty city! For in one hour is thy judgment come. And the merchants of the earth shall weep and mourn over her*; for no man buyeth their merchandise any more . . . . *The merchants of these things, which were made rich by her, shall stand afar off for the fear of her torment, weeping and wailing, and saying, Alas, alas, that great city*, that was clothed in fine linen, and purple, and scarlet, and decked with gold, and precious stones, and pearls! *For in one hour so great riches is come to nought. And every shipmaster, and all the company in ships, and sailors, and as many as trade by sea, stood afar off, and cried when they saw the smoke of her burning*, saying, What city is like unto this great city! *And they cast dust on their heads, and cried, weeping and wailing, saying, Alas, alas, that great city*, wherein were made rich all that had ships in the sea by reason of her costliness! *For in one hour is she made desolate.* Rejoice over her, thou heaven, and ye holy apostles and prophets; *for God hath avenged you on her*.

Other booklets in
The God's Own Word Series

GOD'S OWN WORD
To Those Who Are Mistreated

Chapter Contents
(63 pages)

Do Good to Those Who Mistreat You
Love Your Enemies
Maintain a Tender Heart and
a Forgiving Spirit
Rejoice When You Suffer
for Christ's Sake
Wait with Patience upon the Lord's
Deliverance
Trust the Lord to Repay Those Who
Mistreat You

GOD'S OWN WORD
On Our Fears

Chapter Contents
(80 pages)

Fear Thou Not
Fear in the Midst of Affliction
I Will Fear No Evil
Afraid of Man
Delivered from Fear
Fear as a Judgment from the Lord

www.shepherdingtheflock.com

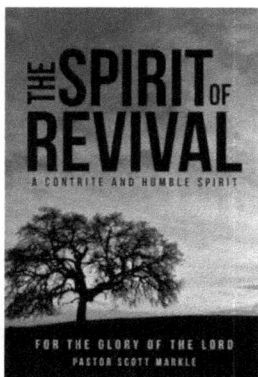

Other books from

Shepherding the Flock Ministries

GOD'S WISDOM For MARRIAGE & the HOME

A comprehensive study of what the Word of God teaches about marriage and the home, including chapters on:
The Priority of Marriage
The Permanency of Marriage
The Purpose of Marriage
Cleaving unto Thy Wife (Parts 1 & 2)
An Help Meet for Him (Parts 1 & 2)
Love One Another
One-Flesh Unity
(446 pages)

THE SPIRIT OF REVIVAL
A CONTRITE AND HUMBLE SPIRIT

A Biblical study of the inseparable relationship between Biblical humility and spiritual revival, including studies in Isaiah 57:15-21; James 4:1-10; 2 Chronicles 7:12-14; Psalm 51:1-19; and Isaiah 66:1-5. *(200 pages)*

www.shepherdingtheflock.com

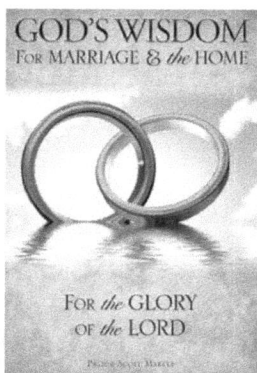

www.ingramcontent.com/pod-product-compliance
Lightning Source LLC
Chambersburg PA
CBHW070551030426
42337CB00016B/2447